To Tim,

much kindness

Jon

The Lost Patriarch

Towards a New Mythology of Manhood

Stephen Duke

Bloomington, IN
authorHOUSE™
Milton Keynes, UK

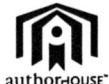

AuthorHouse™
1663 Liberty Drive, Suite 200
Bloomington, IN 47403
www.authorhouse.com
Phone: 1-800-839-8640

AuthorHouse™ UK Ltd.
500 Avebury Boulevard
Central Milton Keynes, MK9 2BE
www.authorhouse.co.uk
Phone: 08001974150

© 2007 Stephen Duke. All rights reserved.

No part of this book may be reproduced, stored in a retrieval system, or transmitted by any means without the written permission of the author.

First published by AuthorHouse 1/30/2007

ISBN: 978-1-4259-4443-8 (sc)

Printed in the United States of America
Bloomington, Indiana

This book is printed on acid-free paper.

Contents

Chapter 1:
Heroes of the Heart — 1

Chapter 2:
Manhood And Sex — 25

Chapter 3:
The Search for Love — 57

Chapter 4:
"Forming Families" — 77

Chapter 5:
"Families Breaking Up" — 137

Chapter 6:
War and Games — 179

Chapter 7:
"The New Male Life Cycle" — 205

Chapter 8:
A Future Vision of Post Patriarchy — 253

CHAPTER 1:
Heroes of the Heart

<u>Manhood and Post Patriarchy</u>

**All men are still patriarchs.
They are struggling to evolve their ancient manhood psychology;
in a new world of POST PATRIARCHY created by women.**

The liberation of women has shattered the old world of patriarchy, in which men have been comfortably living for many thousands of years. Men are now living through an age of revolutionary change in their gender psychology. The consequences and fallout for each individual man are cataclysmic. Men did not start the revolution. In fact they tried as hard as possible to stop it happening. And they failed! Men are now caught up in the global storm of change, and have no real idea or sense of control over where they are being taken by it.

All men are still "natural" patriarchs, living in what is now a <u>post</u> patriarchal culture. As a result, each man's time, is now a lifelong struggle to radically reshape his manhood. Learning to live as men in this new reality, emotionally, sexually, at work with our colleagues and at home with our families, involves fundamental changes in the meaning of manhood.

The challenge now to all men, is to overcome their experience of fear of disempowerment, at the liberating empowerment of women. To do this, they need to allow themselves to celebrate with joy the loving, nurturing and feminine aspect of their own psychology, alongside their competitive, heroic masculinity. By learning to balance in a new harmonious combination, their masculine and feminine "opposites", their manhood can achieve a new wholeness of being. This reinvention of manhood from macho man to post patriarch, could well be the next great step in the psycho-evolutionary story of both our gender and our species.

Men are now having to confront the biggest challenges in their evolutionary history. We are being challenged to immerse ourselves in our feeling, feminine psychology; and discover a new balance in our manhood, between hero and homemaker, tough guy and tender man, provider and nurturer. Our role in the three million year old evolutionary story of manhood, is suddenly being re-written. We are struggling to find ways to understand our confusion and anger, about an event which we did not want and over which we had little or no control.

The basic patterns of the male life cycle are also being changed. A new Male Life Cycle is now emerging

The Lost Patriarch

> In the great plan and pattern of Evolution, all things must change. **Failure to change means failure to adapt. And failure to adapt eventually means: EXTINCTION!!!** So now, in our post feminist, post patriarchal world of the global village, the human genome, a quantum computer and holidays booked in Space, the patriarchal male is due for a radical design overhaul. The current model is **OUTMODED**. It has to be taken back to the evolutionary design studio to be re-imagined, re-thought and re-invented.

One of the first priorities is to take apart and rebuild the fragile structure, that organises so much of our out of date manhood:

Beyond Patriarchy

Some men are beginning to become aware of the enormity of this unfolding change. Most of us still refuse to recognise it. None of us can yet begin to accept it. It means the end of the comfortable fit between what Nature programmed us to do, as the male of the species; and the world of patriarchy that for so long was organised around us.

At home with our families, we are now told to become more attentive to our partners and more nurturing to our children. We are told to abandon and give up many of our more selfish habits; our compulsive hero seeking, an addiction to sport, our male obsession with sex, a preoccupation with our own emotionally narcissistic needs. We are asked to become homemakers and domestic gods. At work we have to learn to accept women executives who can boss us around, and whose professional authority we must obey and respect. Emotionally, we are told we must learn to "open up". Train ourselves to let out all the complex feelings and thoughts by which we are often tormented; self doubt, confusion about our manhood, lack of confidence in our true masculinity and confusion about our roles at work and at home. We are living at a time when nearly all men are experiencing a crisis in **manhood identity.**

At the same time as taking on more emotionally nurturing family roles as homemakers and fathers, we are having to learn to love our female partners in a more generous way. We are trying to do this, but when families break up, we then feel emotionally devastated and cut-off from our children. We struggle to avoid becoming emotionally peripheral to the family circle, in whose centre we worked

The Lost Patriarch

so hard to be. Half of all fathers "cope" with this by cutting off completely with their children, and running away from their emotional devastation, loss and pain.

At the same time, we feel under ever greater pressure from our employers to deliver the goods at work. Despite all this, divorce and family break-up escalates out of control. And while all this psychological meltdown is going on around us, we still remain driven from inside by the most powerful psychological energy of manhood: to find our way to **become a hero and make our own special difference in the world.**

Patriarchy is dead. The old rules no longer apply to "being a man". The only rule about being a man today is:

you can be certain of nothing in an uncertain gender world.

Despite all the apparent chaos, if we can begin to face the changes happening outside around us, and inside ourselves as individual men, we can begin to recognise one thing. Our role as men in a patriarchy **was a very limiting role.** *It kept us locked into just one side or aspect of our total manhood psychology. When we can learn to begin to let ourselves recognise this, we can begin to flow with the new insight of our time. It is providing us with a great opportunity to break out and become something better, deeper, more complex and complete as a human being. In this radical transition through which we are now living, a man can look inwards and make important new self-*

Stephen Duke

discoveries. The opportunity that today's crisis brings, is to tune a man into his richly creative feminine energy, as well as staying connected to his heroic masculine energy. A man has a chance to become a more complete person: hero, provider, homemaker, nurturer and creative man of the spirit.

> **Being a man now, is not just about toughness. Along with the traditional territory of manhood, comes the need to learn and practise tenderness. Toughness and tenderness, softness and strength. Quite a contradictory menu; such a mixed diet. Acquiring the stuff of manhood is no longer a one dimensional task. Nowadays it's harder to learn how to become a man. Perhaps harder than it's ever been: because that's what trying to live as a man in a post patriarchy is all about.**

*A man's feminine side opens up to him the way of new artistic and spiritual creativity: music, painting, writing; all the arts are calling him. He knows the traditional male territories of work, achievement, the sports field, drinking clubs and the pursuit of sex. What he is now so confused about, is how to enter the softer, creative more soulful territories that arrive with his newly released feminine energies. The way forward lies in exploring both with equal interest and discovering a **new balance** and wholeness.*

Portrait of a Man

As I stood next to him on the sports field watching his son, I knew he was unhappy. There is no such thing as an easy divorce. And he was going through his. I went out on a limb and said:

"Love is such a big thing: yet we guys seem to know nothing about it. Until life really hits us in the face: when somebody dies on us, or we go through a divorce "

He looked at me. There was a pause: then to my surprise he said: "You know I think you've got something there. "

Something was opening up in him. He began to talk to me about his **feelings.** He spoke to me about his pain at the loss of his wife, his home and the break up of his family. But strangely he also told me about the joy of seeing more of his two children. He saw more of them now after the break-up, he said, than before when he was living with them. After the break up, he had become more emotionally connected to his intimate family circle of love. The nurturing father had woken up in him.

He and I were standing together as we watched our children running. It was a cross-country race for the local schools. There were hundreds of children there and dozens of couples watching their kids. He was alone.

"I'm still trying to get used to it. Being alone. I like my freedom. But I miss everybody like hell," he said quietly.

"Why is it we have no education about Love? It comes so naturally to women. It's no wonder they get so pissed *off with us. We can't understand their emotional language can we?"*

I had to agree with him. He continued; *"She and I lived in different worlds. I used to get up and go to work all day. It was the only way I believed I could show that I cared. I had to work my bollocks off. In the evening I went out to rugby training; then on a Friday night I had a few beers. On Saturday I played a match. She was angry with me, because I was not emotionally present with her and the kids. I couldn't give her what she wanted because I didn't understand it. Now that it's all fallen apart, it's becoming clearer to me. Like nearly all men,* **I've had no emotional education."**

The Two Great Forces: The Masculine Force

In order to have any chance of beginning to make an improved design of himself, a man needs to begin to be able to see the basic material of which he is made up. He needs to recognise that he emerges out of two entirely different great energies or forces: the **Masculine Force** and the **Feminine Force.** By being born male, he quickly learns to tune into one of these two great forces, the Masculine Force. From the age of around two years old, he begins to play his male part on the stage of Life. From that very early age of two years old, he begins to live as a male in the world. His father, brothers, male friends, male teachers, uncles, all help to 'switch on' and release in him this fundamental masculine force. Role models he discovers on video, in books, TV soaps and films, all activate and release his male potential waiting to emerge. At the same time as this is happening, something psychological comes alive in him, that will stay active in his mind for the rest of his life. He will start to try and learn **how to be a Hero.** The drive, the search, the energy of seeking to be a Hero, is at the very core of a man's masculinity. It is something so deeply instinctive by which he is driven, that we call it an **archetype.** Twenty thousand years ago, it was released and expressed through the elemental struggle for survival, hunting; the hands on killing of animals and bringing home food. Then our need for heroic manhood was further satisfied by belonging to the intimate male group, that painted itself in wild vivid colours and danced horny ecstatic tribal dances, after having snorted hallucinogenic drugs. In the world of today this compulsive archetypal behaviour, is still expressed compulsively in our search for challenges: in the quest for achievement, money, sport and physical conquest, success and the desperate need for recognition by other men. Inside us, very little has changed about that part of our primal psychological inheritance. In childhood it is naturally competitive, seeking out victory over other males on the sports field and in the classroom. Later in our adult manhood, it wants to be dominant in the rivalries and battles we encounter in our workplace. It gains fulfilment by trying to climb the social, business or educational ladders to the top. The masculine force seeks empowerment, dominance, control and a sense freedom.

Stephen Duke

The Feminine Force

The other great energy from which we have to grow ourselves as individual men, as we travel through life, is the Feminine Force. This great Force is as different, as opposite from the Masculine Force as it is possible to be. The more tuned in we become to our masculine energy, the more difficult it is for us to experience and understand the Feminine Force inside us. In complete contrast, it is non aggressive, nurturing, receptive, anti-heroic, intuitive, reflective, imaginative, artistic, musical and spiritual. The Feminine Force tunes us into our generous warm human feelings and is concerned with kindness, compassion and love. The Feminine Force nurtures relationships in their many forms; in the family, in friendships, at work with colleagues, in contact with Nature, within communities and towards other nations and cultures. The Masculine Force tunes us men into our individual, selfish hero quest and seeks out competition, victory and conquest over Nature, over other men, over women, other communities and other nations and tribes. The Feminine Force in supreme contrast, radiates an **energy of union**. The artistic or musical man, (songwriters, poets, painters) speak from the feminine soul through their work. They are moved by their rich creative contact with the Feminine Force. The Feminine Force has an energy of union that brings things and people together, nurturing and sustaining contact and connections between them.

Connecting the Forces

Slowly, over patriarchal time, the male of the species learned to censure and cut off from much of what actually was fresh, healthy, genuine and alive in him. By learning to censor his emotions and switch off his imagination, his manliness became **one dimensional**. It was defined only by his emotional toughness, which meant not showing or permitting himself to have any feelings at all! Living as unemotional macho man, made it extremely difficult and confusing for him to get in touch with and experience his 'other side' or the Feminine Force. He became split off. This 'other side' involved his feelings, his imagination, his tenderness, his artistic and spiritual energies that connected him to the world and the universe. They were qualities of feeling, behaviour and spirit, he learned to mostly identify as belonging to women, "the weaker sex". In psychological terms, they became unconscious in him, and he "gave them away" to women. In our time, women have gained their own liberation, through their connection with the masculine force inside themselves. They have gained a genuine empowerment by being more in touch with both of the great forces; the Feminine Force **and** the Masculine Force.

Feminism has liberated the masculine heroic energy in women.

Now in post patriarchy, a woman seeks more fulfilment of herself through her achieving, masculine side. At the same time when in a relationship with a man, she also expects him to express more of his softer, nurturing, feminine nature. This is the new psychological "exchange" that is currently causing so much confusion and conflict in the male female relationship

Over time in patriarchy, men have actually come to feel more and more like prisoners in the world, split off from their other side. It is time now for the post patriarchal man to 'come out'. So the first and most important principle in the re design of the post patriarchal male, is to grow a deeper understanding of the opposite but complementary sides to his psychological manhood.

Making this deep connection for the post patriarchal male, is not straight forward. The signs and symptoms of the deep inner conflict that currently affects men, are very visible: delinquency, depression, psychiatric illness and suicide amongst young men is at its highest ever in this country. Divorce or break up with partners and family, has a profound emotional scarring on men. It now affects the vast majority of men at some time in their lives. We are a gender oppressed by alcohol abuse, sex and drug addiction; we inflict violence towards women, children and other men. We are unhappy with our work and suffer from a loss of faith or vision in our future. We have become a **gender out of balance.**

Disconnection of the Head and Heart

For a long time now, a man from a very early age, has learned to keep his emotions, his imagination and even his thoughts, under control and hidden from view. Rather than *being a fault or a problem, this 'manliness' became identified as his strength. It has become valued as one core aspect of his 'manliness'.*

> **There are clear signs however, that this disconnection of head and heart, is showing signs of extreme wear and tear. Men are breaking down in alarming numbers with ill health, both physical and psychological. Many men feel trapped behind a wall of confusion, isolation and self-doubt. The true identity of what being a man in the 21st century is all about remains hidden from them.**

The problems of ' Being a Man '

In our country we men like to think of ourselves as part of The Bull –Dog Breed. By doing that, we men can tune into something inside ourselves that has the ruggedness and toughness of the bull-dog. The bulldog spirit helps us celebrate our manhood in our many manly competitive and physical activities; football, rugby, boxing, running, climbing mountains, exploring, etc. Winston Churchill, who led us to victory through one of the darkest passages in our history, possessed the **"bull-dog spirit.**"*For us it is a* **symbol of**

manhood. *The bulldog, symbolises the pure, primal, brutal strength which burns like molten lava inside each of us men. This primal strength glows with an unconquerable, timeless energy. It enables us to run, fight, climb, compete, endure and overcome challenges that would terrify and otherwise overwhelm us. A man tunes into this primal survival energy, when confronted with extreme circumstances. Emerging battered and wounded, bleeding but victorious from his confrontation with a fearful challenge, a man gains a deep* **sense of heroism.** *His manly pride, his machismo, is flattered and fulfilled. In Spain the supreme machismo challenge is to enter the ring and actually to fight with the bull. Here, it is to run onto the pitch driven by the bulldog spirit, and defeat the All Blacks at Twickenham, score the goal that wins the World Cup, or stroke the winning runs at Lords to regain the Ashes against the Old Enemy. In both cultures, Spanish and Anglo Saxon, the manhood psychology is the same. Each man joyfully engages his primal inner strength with a brutal external battle, in pursuit of conquest, victory and fulfilment of his innate* **heroism and machismo.**

We men have always lived at our most vivid when encountering challenges. Now, like before in our history, we again have a great challenge facing us. It involves the primal energies of the bulldog, the wildman, and the hero-adventurer that still live vividly inside us. However, this new challenge, also involves learning to connect and celebrate the opposite, softer, feminine energies that also live inside us.

The supreme challenge we now face, is to learn more how to **balance** *these* **"opposite"** *energies, and so become more whole and complete in our evolving manhood.*

A Crisis of Manhood Identity

It is not an easy time to be a man. Epidemics of mental and physical illness are rife throughout the western world. It is also fair to say that many millions of men between the age of 20-50 are in the experience we can only describe as a crisis of manhood identity. These are the common questions to which they are all currently struggling to find answers:

Is my Manhood okay?
What does Manhood mean?
Am I doing well enough at work?
How can I do better?
Am I a good enough father?
How do I become a better one?
What kind of role model am I to my son?
What kind of man does my partner want or need me to be?
Is domestic democracy possible between her and me?
What does that mean for our family roles?
What does that mean for our work roles?
Will my partner and I stay together?
Is it okay if she earns more than me, or do I need to earn more than her?

Stephen Duke

How "successful " do I need to be?
How can I find a Work-Life Balance?
What is my life for?
Do I need to be stronger or softer?
Do I have a spiritual side?

Accompanying these many specific questions that will regularly come into the mind of most men, are their accompanying feelings and emotions. These tend to be negative emotions, most commonly anxiety, fear, sadness, mild depression, guilt, self doubt, hostility and anger. It is important that we recognise that so many of us men, from time to time experience these feelings. We need to understand that they are a symptom of the current crisis of manhood identity. We should describe them as normal. It is the sign of the times, the current state of the male mind; what men are about in the world of today. These difficult negative emotions are much of what the male life journey is currently so much about. From the moment we can start to admit this to ourselves, things can start to get better. There is a sense of relief that we are "normal"; even that we are probably doing okay and well enough. Also we can start to have a sense of connection with other men. We can begin to see ourselves connected to a much larger process or collective male psychology, inside and outside ourselves, which we all are sharing

The 21st Century journey of manhood is through this time of uncertainty, towards a very different future of manhood. By identifying the pattern of which we are now a part, we make connections, inside ourselves and with others. This begins a process of empowerment and conscious change for each one of us. It begins to move us toward an improved awareness of what kind of man we want to be, and the kind of manhood we admire. An important aspect of this, is the ability to take better care of ourselves: to nurture ourselves through this process of change. From there we can continue the ongoing personal growth in a time of challenge. Today just being a man, in a time of so much uncertainty, is an heroic journey in itself.

The Search for a More Balanced Manhood.

What is it like if a man allows his life to become more of a search for the New Balance? How does he begin to go about this? Where will the search lead him? What are the benefits for him, for his partner, his children and work colleagues?

In the search for a new kind of balance, what he is exploring is a new wholeness of being. In doing this he does not have to abandon or give away, any of the core elements of his masculinity. He does not have to **shrink himself in any way.** *Instead he has to learn to release and* **expand himself.** *By expanding, by growing out emotionally, he starts to liberate himself. He liberates himself from a way of thinking, feeling and behaving that belonged to the patriarchal past, and by which his potential for wholeness was imprisoned. The challenge for men, is to soften the brittleness of their masculinity, and tune into* *their 'other side'. This is very difficult to do, because like all radical change, it is a leap into the unknown. It creates fear, insecurity and anxiety. Here are some of the opposites, men will need to try and explore, in their search to discover their new balance of manhood.*

PROVIDER or NURTURER
DOMINANCE or CO-EQUALITY?
GIVER OF LOVE and TAKER OF LOVE
EMOTIONAL DETACHMENT
or
EMOTIONAL INVOLVEMENT?

Exercise. Think about how you can live with these opposites in a more in balanced way, in these three key areas of your life:

FAMILY –WORK-FRIENDS

What I am proposing here for the man of the future, is a vision of how he can begin his radical re modelling and re-designing. It looks forward to a time when a man no longer defines himself as a man, in a purely one dimensional way; i.e. tough/brittle, in control, power seeking, domineering, compulsively competitive and emotionally blocked and tight lipped. I am going to describe a radical re-invention of ourselves as men, **that can adapt to the changes that have occurred around us.** *How do we go about it?*

The Lost Patriarch

Changes in Women

POWER GIRL

Strange as it may seem, psychologically feminism was a very **masculine** *movement. This is because it enabled women to tune into the Masculine Force. The song, "Search for the hero inside yourself" is sung by a woman to other women. Women now go off in pursuit of their own heroism. Becoming a nurturer is not an heroic ambition for the post feminist female. Another song : "Sisters are doin' it for themselves", makes the message absolutely clear. Stand aside guys and let the women in. In the education system in our country, women now out achieve men up until they enter University and often beyond. In many of the big companies and businesses, women play a leadership and management role at the highest level. It is a woman who currently holds the world record for the fastest sailing solo trip around the world. Women are finding leading positions in politics, business, science, sport; and this is only the beginning! Women have achieved this over only* **the last**

Stephen Duke

two generations. *What will they have done in another ten generations? Another five hundred years? For women and therefore for us men, the world has changed:* **forever!!**

In a police detective series on British television in the '90's, called Prime Suspect, the main character was a high ranking female detective. In an early scene from the first episode, she was brought in by the assistant chief constable and introduced to the large team of other detectives on the case. She had been chosen to lead the team; they were all men. For what seemed an age, the camera panned slowly across the faces of the long line of men who stood in dumbfounded silence as they received the news. Masterfully, the actors showed the full range of emotions on their stricken silent faces, that men have felt at the growing empowerment of women in the workplace: shock, disbelief, hostility, fear, shame, humiliation, anger, rebellion, fight back. The involvement and self empowerment of women in the workplace, has challenged the identity of men at a core level of their masculinity: the hero. For thousands of years in patriarchy, men have expressed their need to be heroes, by playing the role of the provider/patriarch. That unique role for men has now gone. Women can provide for themselves when they want to; they need men financially less and less. Feminism has liberated them to release and express their heroic achieving energy; and they are getting better and better at it. Remember, the world has changed forever; because we now live in a post patriarchy. In a post patriarchy, the two most important roles that human beings play in human culture, Provider and Nurturer, are now up for grabs by both genders. No one gender has an exclusive right to either of them any more.

Male Liberation

What does Male Liberation mean?

Emotional recovery into a new psychological health and wholeness
Learning to celebrate the new duality of Nurturer and Provider roles
Re-engagement with the deep masculine archetypal Hero energy
in parallel with engagement with the new feminine
Escape from two generations of being confused followers
into becoming clear headed leaders again.

For the last two generations, men have fought a rearguard **reaction against** *the liberation initiatives taken by women. Now they can understand, that after women's liberation, can follow their own* **male liberation***. Their machismo and primal manhood will always be validated, so long as they continue to pursue their own hero path. However, by also validating themselves equally as nurturers and embracing the feminine in their psychology, the old-fashioned gender war, will become a human condition of our evolutionary* past. When men learn to make this psycho-evolutionary leap, then the man and woman of the future can become the **Co-Equal Couple.**

The man and woman of the future, will be able to interchange the masculine roles of hero/heroine, male achiever/power girl with the feminine roles of nurturer/parent. Research shows that nearly two thirds of men are ready to do this, by taking more time off to be with and nurture their children and be more in the home. The current disturbance in the male female relationship needs to be brought to an end. The future belongs to the Co-Equal Couple, who share with equal satisfaction and fulfilment a balanced relationship, in the home and out in the world. Men and women at work each can face their own challenges. To achieve this fundamental shift in the new psychology of manhood, the futureman has to embrace and take ownership of a broad aspect of the feminine within himself. Hidden and concealed from him in the past, by his machismo and traditional manhood role in patriarchy, the futureman can now become truly liberated.

Male Portraits

1.LEXUS MAN: An interesting case of machismo

Lexus Man is the overdriven 'A Type' male, powered by a need to obliterate all competition and rivals. He must take on and overcome all challenges he sees before him. When a success in business, this could be ok for him and us: but

The Lost Patriarch

business success alone, cannot satisfy his power seeking dominating male ego. He needs constantly and repeatedly to proclaim his achievements to all and sundry, and if no when else is present, yet again to his all enduring and submissive wife. At every opportunity his trumpet must be overblown, screaming to us its melody of self adulation. His ego knows virtually no bounds and can be restrained, only a little, by his few lifetime male companions. He is John Wayne's western hero, reincarnated in the post modern material world. If you play off 16, he plays off eight. If your money is in gilts, he is speculating in high risk biotechs. He cannot sit still: a garden is something to be instantly re-engineered, dug up. His lawn must be relayed in wood, concrete and stone. Above all, Nature must be controlled: a divine Nature, with whose soft elemental forces he has lost contact. The green man inside him can be lived only via projection. That is to say, he will be interested in the gentleness of other men, and not really know why. These men are his other side, his shadow psychology that still follows him around. Somehow, it rings a bell, whose quiet, insistent toll, he cannot completely ignore. Southern Spain or Portugal is his lifelong destination, his personal Shangri La, where the outmoded English class system, and its distaste for the overstated and showy, cannot cramp his exhibitionist style. There men can still be men, and the sun never sets on the hero who wants still to be all things.

CHAPTER 2:
Manhood And Sex

The Twin Gods of Sex

THE RAMPANT INNER SEX GOD

There lives is inside each one of us males, a Rampant Inner Sex God. He has a primeval energy and has emerged with us, from our ancient and pagan past. Images of him appear in cultures all around the planet; typically as the god of male fertility. Ancient paintings and murals depict his male seed, combining with Nature and the seasons. His fertility enables the crops to grow and flourish. In our modern context, he fuels us with high-octane, raw sexual energy and free flowing testosterone. The Rampant Inner Sex God is without moral scruples or human emotional loyalties. He is the sexual under lord of male machismo. We experience him as a wild lust demon. **His emotional intelligence is non-existent.** That is, he can make no apparent connection between caring emotions and his riotous sexual desires.

> **The Rampant Inner Sex God prevents men developing their *loving intelligence*.**

He is the sexual demon who can successfully sabotage our attempts to achieve any lasting relationship with a woman. This can only be achieved by learning to respect, to receive trust, offer empathy, show attentiveness, being kind and generous towards our female companion. The rampant sex god sabotages all of this. He is the opposite of the loving that sustains.

The rampant inner sex god is the proud stag, the lord of the forest, the corn god of Nature. His raw sexual energy is beautiful, powerful, ecstatic and sublime. In pre-Christian times, he was acknowledged as sacred. His energy was released in religious orgiastic rituals. Even today, he reminds us that male sexuality is more than testosterone or chemicals. The sex god is a primal **psychological** energy.

He is a supreme psychological force, vibrating, pulsating; an erotic force constantly alive inside us. Unless we are careful to master him, he will take over and be destructive of our lives. Remember the president who almost lost all of it for a blowjob?

The rampant inner sex god is amoral, wildly promiscuous, and his sexual hunger literally cannot be satisfied. He is there to fertilise the feminine in Nature. He seeks out and desires all around him. He is restless and remorseless and without shame. He is the most elemental, primal and ancient power in our manhood psychology. We inherit him as a godlike force that celebrates our sexual strength and power. He also seeks control and mastery.

The Rampant Inner Sex God, is not just about sex. If we are properly connected to him, he helps us tune into the most fiery, unconquerable masculine part of ourselves. He is essential to our psychological well being. How do we both stay tuned into him but not mastered by him? This is not so easy in the world of today. He is very unfashionable with the contemporary post feminist woman. He unbalances the co-equal couple in the bedroom. Fortunately, we are helped by another sex god to control his extremes.

Stephen Duke

The Love Prince

THE LOVE PRINCE

In complete and sublime contrast to the Rampant Inner Sex God, we also have someone very different inside us: The Love Prince. The Love Prince is very special. He is light, beautiful and feels divine. When we allow ourselves to experience his energy in the company of a woman, we are lifted up out of our everyday selves. He is deeply romantic and likes to give service; he willingly provides favours. He sends flowers, and is inspired to write poetry. He is tender and worships a woman's beauty and sexuality. It is the Love Prince that makes sex beautiful, even sacred between us and our lady. He seeks to provide sexual favours to her and be in her sexual service. He gets pleasure by giving pleasure. It is his energy that makes us generous and attentive lovers. The Love Prince is switched on by the falling-in-love experience. He comes alive in us when we meet the "right lady." Something magical, alchemical and holy, comes alive in the field of energy between her and us, and then the

The Lost Patriarch

Love prince appears. Whereas the Rampant Inner Sex God is horny, hot, domineering, demanding, lustful and greedy, the Love Prince is kind, gentle, nurturing, attention giving, romantically passionate and loving. In his own very different way, the Love Prince is irresistible to the opposite sex. In matters of sex and love making, he is the other side of the twin gods that compose our male sexuality. The post feminist lady probably desires her male sexual partner to be 90% love prince, with the latent potential to play the rampant sex god on 10% of occasions!

"MALE SEXERCISE"

Which are you more: Love Prince or Rampant Sex God?
How often do you become one?
How often do you become the other?
What do you do and say when you feel Rampant Sex God?
What do you do and say when you feel Love Prince?
Is there a way for you to combine both more often?
Which does your lady prefer?
When does she prefer it?
What does she ask you to do for her as Rampant Sex God?
What does she ask you to do as Love Prince?

The Rampant Inner Sex God and the Love Prince embrace the two wide polarities of our male sexuality. We should learn and come to know them well. Each different lady, with whom we have intimate relationships, switches on one or the other. By the Rampant Inner Sex God, we can be persuaded that the whole thing can only be about sex. By the Love Prince we can follow her around as a doting fool, enslaved in her romantic service. Growing up sexually, means finding a relationship in which we can play both roles often enough, to release their contrasting forces and energies. In this way we harmonise them with a life empowering creativity and balance.

Manhood, Sex and the Male Orgasm

Sex, orgasm and manhood are all combined together in some fundamentally important way. The loss of male virginity, has always been associated with actual or approaching manhood. Virility and initiation rites have long been a psychological entry into manhood. Can you recall your "first time" and what arrived afterwards? An amazing sense of joy and release, of achievement and completion, all combined. Then following on from that, a strong sense of belonging now to the world of men. It is interesting that one of the principle ways that we enter the world of manhood, is through experiencing sexual intimacy with a woman.

The loss of our sexual virginity, is a key moment psychologically in the life of any male. Something inside us is recognised, that is profoundly important in the gaining and *reinforcement of our male identity. It is achieved through performing the act of sex and orgasm. I emphasise sex and orgasm, because orgasm is the natural fulfilment of our sex drive. As male teenagers we will be involved in a good deal of solitary fantasy sex and self giving pleasure. These can both result in ejaculation and climax; but neither of them achieve or result in* **orgasm.** *Male orgasm requires the actual penetration of a female, and therefore being taken in and willingly received inside of her. To achieve this we have to be erect and firm. Our penis has to be swollen and big. Our male sexuality has become turned on, tuned in and fully activated. Aroused in this way we are totally and sexually male. This creates for us a natural sense of pride in our masculine beauty and wholeness. We celebrate sexually our masculine power. Our first orgasm with a female, affirms and reinforces our experience of becoming a young man and achieving manhood.*

In our first sexual union, our female partner is open and receptive to us. As we instinctively penetrate and rhythmically thrust into her, our strong sexual energy raises her level of excitement. As we thrust and move inside her, this increasingly turns on and tunes in her sexual energy. Male and female, Yin and Yang, entering and receiving, combine in an erotic dance that satisfies each of the two genders. This is a primal and fundamental act in Nature: entry of the female by the male. On that first occasion and from then on, we begin to learn how to experience ourselves as part of that universal process of union, between the male and female.

Sex at this developmental stage in young manhood, has an intense urgency towards release, completion and orgasm. As we become more experienced in sex, we learn techniques and skills that restrain and control that urgency to orgasm. In our early days of sexual activity, we have little self-control over this overwhelming urge to ejaculation and orgasm. When a man's orgasm arrives, it can best be described as an explosive loss of control. A man "comes". Something arrives and carries him away. He arrives somewhere else. He physically ejaculates his sperm, shooting off his biological seed into the woman. Whilst that is happening, he simultaneously experiences a transient ecstatic pleasure. This is accompanied by an intensely powerful emotional release. He moans and screams uncontrollably; or he shouts out his partner's name, proclaims his love for her. Male sexual orgasm is a compelling experience of self-abandonment, and transcendent ecstasy. Psychologically, our separate masculinity momentarily disappears. Just for a few moments a man falls without control, into an erotic sea of bliss and union with the feminine. In these few brief moments, he may lose completely any sense of himself and becomes merged with his partner. Psychologically as well as physically, he fuses with the feminine. He disappears into the woman's ocean of welcome and receptiveness. He is no longer a separate individual man, but is merged momentarily in an ecstatic connection with the feminine.

He has gone into his lady, his love goddess/earth mother and momentarily becomes lost in her. In these few thrilling moments of orgasm, he has given away his sperm, (his biogenetic map) and lost his desire for separateness.

In the early days of reaching sexual manhood, a man associates his virility with repeated orgasms. The more orgasms and the more women he has them with, seems to satisfy his longing to discover and express his sexual machismo. The Rampant Sex God is very active at this stage of his sexual development! Very high levels of testosterone in our teenage years and twenties, is the bio-chemical engine for the male sex drive at this life stage. There is a long tradition in patriarchy, of emerging manhood being realised by multiple sexual conquests. A young man longs for erotic experience with the female of the species, whenever and wherever he finds them.

Slowly, things change for us. The urgency to orgasm and early sexual release, becomes more controllable. We begin to enjoy penetration of our female partner, for much longer periods before reaching orgasm. We gather sexual experience and become more practised and skilful sexual practitioners. Psycho- sexually the Rampant Sex God, begins to learn to live with The Love Prince! This results in us becoming more conscious of the physical and sexual needs of our female partner. Sex becomes more of a mutual erotic dance, than an impulsive act of self fulfilment.

As our testosterone levels gradually reduce and we grow older, we gain much more control in managing our orgasms.

Stephen Duke

We can even learn to have long periods of penetrative sex without orgasm. The oriental system recommends this whenever possible. But it is a struggle of self-control and self discipline for a man, whatever his age, to manage his impulsive desire for sexual release and orgasm. We still want to complete sex with orgasm.

There are two main elements of the male orgasmic experience, that satisfy and reward a man. Firstly it releases the intense physical arousal energy inside him, that is activated by bio-chemical interaction and the increase of sexual hormones in his body. This physical, chemical and hormonal energy peaks at the moment of orgasmic experience. It has a natural urgency and intense flow towards climax and completion. This can only be achieved through ejaculation inside a female. Secondly and psychologically, his male identity is profoundly reinforced by the experience of orgasm. This is paradoxical because at the actual moment of orgasmic release, his separate masculine identity is momentarily surrendered as he falls into the universal sea of the feminine inside his partner. When he emerges he feels more of a man. The orgasm experience itself, is one of the male rites of passage and a form of self-initiation that enables us to feel like a man. Each experience of orgasm is a consummate experience of our self, as a man. It is also, simultaneously a sublime connection with the spiritual and cosmic feminine. In an age without God, our brief, blissful encounter with orgasm, can provide some sort of transient divine union, for which we men all still long. This fleeting experience of orgasmic heaven, is for many of us, the nearest we can now get (without drugs), to an experience of the transcendent and divinely feminine.

Oral Sex: The Man's View

On average, a woman's clitoris has twice the number of pleasure receptors than the number on a man's penis head

Even in an age of so-called sexual freedom and enlightenment, the clitoris remains for many men, a small female organ of great sexual mystery. It often remains so throughout much, most or all of their sexual lives. Even after forty years or more of sexual liberation for both genders, men do not seem comfortable talking openly to one another about the clitoris. Breasts or bottom talk amongst men comes easy; the clitoris is more elusive to discuss, even uncomfortable for them. This continued mystification of the clitoris, is even more inexplicable, after two generations of self-proclaimed sexual liberation and feminism by women. Men and women still cannot talk that easily and frankly together, about the sexual organ that can provide women with their most satisfying sexual experiences. Research reveals that 50% of women can achieve female orgasm through clitoral stimulation alone, without penetration or stimulation by a man's penis. Or a woman will reach orgasm while enjoying both at once. Women are increasing their own sexual self-knowledge, and are consequently becoming more instructive and more demanding of men, about how they wish them to satisfy their female sexual needs and desires. Men have to learn to listen more to what women want to tell them, particularly about their clitoral pleasure seeking.

The clitoris is an organ of delicacy and sensuality. It is mostly invisible to the naked eye, for two reasons. Firstly, most of the clitoris is an internal organ; secondly the external tip is hidden under a hood called the prepuce, similar to a man's foreskin. In contrast, a man's penis is always openly visible. When the penis becomes swollen and erect, it stands up in its full glory for all to behold. The clitoris when properly stimulated, also fills with blood and become erect, in similar fashion to the penis. This increases immensely its sensitivity to touch, and its potential for providing erotic pleasure to a woman (and a man). I have used the words delicacy and sensitivity, in describing the clitoris. And it is these words that connect the clitoris with the delights for a woman of receiving oral sex from a man. The soft tendons of a man's tongue are able to provide the clitoris of a woman with more subtle and arousing sensations, than any other part of his body. It is able to provide her with the delicate, sensitive and varied stimulation it requires, in order for her to experience her full and delightful range of oral pleasures. Many women respond to and enjoy oral sex from a man, perhaps more than any other form of sex he can help her experience. This remains a great sexual challenge to men. Men grow up naturally selfish in their sexual pleasure seeking, driven compulsively more by the Rampant Sex God.

Beginning to learn about the pleasure needs and pleasure seeking of his lady partner, is part of a young man's growing up and tuning into his The Love Prince. Both sexually and emotionally, this is essential for him to do.

A man and a woman are a love making system. Perhaps all men should be prepared to attend oral sex seminars; that might be a way forward to improve the male female relationship, if not overnight, then in a short space of time. A woman's responsive delight at receiving her pleasure from a man, activates his pleasure at giving it to her. The erotic circle flows around and between them. This stimulates each other's arousal and response systems even further.

We know as men, that the penis has been celebrated in every form of erotic, religious and secular art for ageless generations. It is symbolic of male prowess, virility, fertility and machismo. It is also understood by men, (and women), to be the ultimate male pleasure organ. When stimulated orally by a woman's mouth, erotic pleasure for a man can be taken to special heights. There are good psychological and physiological reasons for this. Oral sex is an act of extreme sexual generosity and affection, that can only take place when the receiver allows himself or herself to be fully open and vulnerable to the giver. A man stands proud and feels his male sexuality fully affirmed, when a woman administers her fallatio to him. She goes down on him in a literal sense and he feels adored and worshipped by her, fulfilled in his masculine prowess. His bigness stands out for her to touch, suck and adore. In a very real psychological sense when this happens, a man feels **a living sex god.** The sexual god that is always alive in him and ready to become fully awakened, celebrates being worshipped by her service and adoration. A man can also help train his partner in her oral/fellatio skills. He can help her find ways to stimulate him with her mouth and tongue, by identifying those special points on the penis head and body that are the source of his full erotic pleasures. He helps her learn how to co-ordinate her lips and tongue with an effective sucking and rhythmic movement. Can she take the penis deep enough into her mouth to fully satisfy him? There is a moment 5 or 6 seconds before ejaculation, called orgasmic inevitability, when a man cannot not come. This is important for him in his /their decision-making. A man may have a female partner who wishes him to ejaculate in her mouth. Some women see it as part of the total pleasure giving to their male partner. This is an issue of intimate giving and receiving, that provides total fulfilment for partners enjoying oral sex.

Sex and the Erotic Muse.

At the beginning of the film Shakespeare in Love we meet Will Shakespeare. He is a down and out playwright/actor, (not a very distinguished career in 16th century England.) To make matters worse for Will, our hero, he is suffering from a bad case of creative constipation or writer's block. To make life even worse for Will, he has a very fashionable and fantastically handsome rival Christopher Marlowe, who has just had a hugely successful hit in the London theatre. The two of them meet in a trendy Elizabethan bar, and do *a creative war dance around each other. They chat about life and the despair of writing plays for a living. Will has to pretend to his successful rival that he has a new project on the go, and that his pen is hot with creativity. He has a title for his new play: Romeo and Ethel! His rival knows it doesn't sound right for a title of a new play about romance, and by now he is sensing the bullshit that Will is giving him. They say goodbye to each other. Having had to lie to keep up appearances, only leaves Will even more depressed about his barren writer's block. Will writes plays for his travelling theatre company, and the director is beginning to get impatient for the next new play. All around him the pressure is building up, and Will is in real despair. Enter the female Muse. She appears in the form of a beautiful female aristocrat. She comes to his emotional, sexual and creative rescue. He simultaneously falls in love with her, and is also cast under her creative spell. He lives out over a very short period, an amazingly erotic affair. The sex between them is transcendent. It takes him onto a new level of experience and lovemaking. He is enchanted and intoxicated by her beauty and spirit. It is both a physical and spiritual affair between them of great passion and intensity. The fact that she belongs to a socially superior upper class, only makes her power to enchant him even stronger. She is his love goddess and the uptown girl combined. She also falls for him on a big way. She, meanwhile, is being pressured into an arranged marriage with a toadying aristocrat, for whom she feels nothing but contempt. One morning, after* a night of furious and passionate lovemaking with his muse, Will returns home. He picks up his pen and suddenly, hey presto! He starts to write. From then on, he is once again himself; the creative, imaginative playwrighting genius. He cleverly turns into fiction all that he has been living out with his Muse, into his brilliant new play. His female muse has brought alive inside him again, his creative genius. The play he now completes, Romeo and Juliet, is a tribute to the muse. The plot, the poetry, the whole play is inspired by knowing and experiencing his transcendent erotic affair with her.

A muse is a living goddess who inspires a man. She brings out the best of "the other side", in a man. More importantly, it is through meeting and falling for her, **that he finds better things inside himself.** She leads him on to more. There is a special alchemy between a man and his female muse. Beethoven wrote his Moonlight Sonata, for a beautiful young pianist with whom he had fallen in love. As his muse, she had released something very special from inside of him. John Lennon composed his beautiful hymn to the female called "Woman ", inspired by his relationship with Yoko Ono. John Lennon's love for Yoko, also inspired him to compose his most spiritual songs, that called for a new era of peace for Man. Painters spend much of their time trying to paint the perfect female body; their muse. Men are intoxicated with and by the muse.

In their patriarchal past, the vast majority of men, were blocked off from their own rich emotional, imaginative *and spiritual life. Patriarchy oppressed women and simultaneously imprisoned men. By falling in love with his muse, an emotionally unintelligent man (who had learned by conditioning experience, to close off and stifle his inner emotional life), might suddenly start writing and reading reams of poetry. The woman-muse that we come to know erotically, wakes up in a man, his own existing spirit of the creatively feminine. All men have this spirit of the creatively feminine waiting to explode into life inside them. This leads me to the inevitable conclusion that* **all men are naturally feminine.**

The woman-muse unlocks this deeply feminine energy inside a man. Patriarchal man banished it from his conscious mind. From the moment it emerges, and from then on throughout the rest of his life, a man can learn to celebrate in harmony the exquisitely feminine with the riotously masculine. The opportunity and challenge to a men now is more clear: how can they spend the rest of their lives exploring and holding these "opposites" together in greater harmony, and in a new balance? This is one of the great opportunities of the coming time of the post patriarchy, when **men no longer have to be just full time heroes!**

The woman-muse we come to know erotically, changes our masculinity in a way that is profound and compelling. She enchants us, and through that enchantment we discover the locked up feminine inside ourselves. This can be a shock, to which it may take us time to become accustomed. We may feel a temporary loss of emotional balance and self control in our life. We can become a little obsessed with our muse. She has an archetypal energy, a force that will take us over at times, almost like a mental seizure. It is compelling and irresistible. Through knowing her, (in every sense), we have suddenly to learn to live more in touch with the Yin (the feminine) as well as the Yang (the masculine) in our male psychology. It can take us time to regain a sense of control and management of our being in the world and our lives.

Finding our muse has to be a positive and good thing for a man. We should experience it, and learn to celebrate the experience for all its delight and power. We can grow immensely as a man through having the experience. A man who has not found his muse is an incomplete fellow. There is one more thing our muse does for us. She helps us get closer to Nature again. She draws us into our instinctive desire to connect with the soft elemental beauty of Nature and its thousand flowers. Because of our 21st century lifestyle, and the increasingly technological and materialistic culture in which we now live, there is very real danger that our masculine psychology is being driven further and further away from Nature. That can only result in us becoming more unhappy, and experiencing a deep sense of inner alienation from what we are as men. Finding and understanding the language of love for our muse, can play a vital part in helping us satisfy our need to stay in a soulful contact with Nature.

Sex and Marriage

Marriage and sex do not have a happy history. Many marriages that begin to go wrong psychologically, will involve a third sexual partner outside the marriage. When a child arrives, the sexual relationship between the couple is put under pressure. Research shows that couples are often at their most sexually unfulfilled, in the early years of parenthood, when their energies need to be so active elsewhere. This comes as a shocking surprise, most often to the man. A previously intense and fulfilling sexual relationship will suddenly stop, interrupted by the late stage of pregnancy and following childbirth. The bodily changes of pregnancy, childbirth, breast feeding and mothering a new born child, all combine to radically affect a woman's hormonal cycle and balance. Inevitably her and therefore the couples' sexual relationship will be temporarily suspended. Many couples who come to therapy with sexual difficulties, will identify their origin following the birth of their last child.

Many married couples can also arrive in the therapy room with an imbalance in their **interest** in sex. With older couples, after years of a long-term marriage together (more than ten by today's definition of long term), the problems tend to focus around interest, arousal and frequency. Good mutually fulfilling sex and marriage over time, often struggle to go together. Why?

When a married man and a woman arrive at therapy together, sex is usually one of the areas of communication difficulty between them. Usually sex is a physical symptom of *their emotional and psychological struggle for compatibility as a couple. In is not unusual for a man however, although in an emotionally unhappy marriage, still to continue to seek more sex than his female partner. The male sex gods are reluctant to lie low! It seems that a man will often continue to seek and demand sex, even when the emotional breakdown between himself and his wife/partner is serious. Women who are emotionally unhappy in a marriage, are generally the first to begin to lose interest in sex with their male partner. Sex then can frequently become a major source of conflict between them. In this way conflict over sex, can become a physical diversion away from the more serious emotional and gender issues for a couple: e.g. co-equality, life roles, powers of negotiation, responsibility sharing, decision making, co-parenting and nurture/provider roles within the marriage.*

As a man-woman relationship develops and lasts over time in a marriage, sustaining a mutually fulfilling sexual intimacy, often becomes more and more of a challenge for them. At the outset, when a couple are most sexually compatible, it is easy. As time goes on, it gets increasingly difficult for them. The problem is when their individual needs for sex and orgasm become out of balance. The earthly sexual energies of the Rampant Inner Sex God and the romantic longings of The Love Prince to pleasure his Love Goddess, all combine to make up a man's potent sexuality. The typical male has an active and contact seeking interest in sex. In a real and compelling way, he is driven

The Lost Patriarch

by his sex drive. If he cannot "have sex" as often as he wants, he experiences disappointment and frustration with his partner. There are a number of options when he feels like this.

He can work work harder and with more subtlety and generosity, to switch on his female partner sexually. The most common sexual complaint from women, is that men rush through the arousal stage of sex. Seeking their own urgent orgasmic release, they fail to take time to pleasurably arouse their female partner's body. Married men perhaps, can be especially guilty of this.

A married man can masturbate as often as he feels the need, when his partner is sexually unavailable. Marriage and masturbation is still a little shrouded in confusion or guilt. Masturbation for married men; good or bad thing to do? Undoubtedly good!

A sexually frustrated married man can embrace the Chinese way of thinking about male orgasm. The oriental concept of Chi (libido) argues that sexual Chi or energy should be kept inside the body, where it will improve general health and well being. A man who avoids orgasm, will enjoy the longer term benefits of his sexual energy (chi) staying in is body, and contributing to his overall general good health.

A woman's oestrogen levels, may significantly influence her interest in sex. (Hormones again!). When her oestrogen is high, so is her interest in sex. Her monthly ovulation cycle means that her oestrogen level is highest when she is

Stephen Duke

ovulating. Nature programmes a woman to make her most actively interested in sex, when she is most likely to conceive. So a man needs to know what stage of her monthly cycle, his partner is currently experiencing. He needs to take his sexual opportunities well. His need for orgasm is sustained, ongoing, more or less constant. A woman's can naturally be more cyclical. In the longer relationship of a marriage, this natural pattern can become more accentuated.

The 3 Stages of Lovemaking

It is possible for marriage to be good for sex. By sharing a unique sex life together over a number of years, a man and a woman can become more and more tuned into their personal pleasures and erogenous zones. A man and a woman who remain sexual friends, can also allow themselves to become increasingly experimental in their sexual pleasure seeking with each other. To achieve this, a man needs to grow his understanding and awareness of the 3 stages of lovemaking:

Stage 1=Interest   **Stage 2=Arousal**
Stage3= Performance.

STAGE 1=INTEREST:

opening communications can begin about whether either partner is thinking about physical contact/lovemaking. What are the energy levels of each partner? Do they want to go to bed and go straight to sleep? Are they more interested in listening to the radio or reading a book? Or perhaps do they want to talk more about the day that has just happened? How do you check out **Interest?** *(Stage 1)*

A communication rating scale for a couple, ranging from 0 to 3, is very helpful to a couple at the opening of negotiations.

O =NO INTEREST. *Go to sleep; all I want is a cuddle and leave my sexual areas alone!*

1 = MAYBE . *I could be persuaded; but I can take it or leave it.*

2= INTERESTED. *When are we going to do something about it?*

3= HOT FOR IT. *Why are you waiting?!*

(You can add a category of 4, but by the time you start talking about it, you have got your clothes off and are doing all sorts of very sexy things to each other!!)

STAGE 2=AROUSAL.

This is the extended period of sexual contact between a man and a woman, that can last from a few minutes to many hours. If one night in bed, you are checking out your married partner and discover she is on a 2 (strong interest), it should be plain sailing to move from stage 1 Interest, to stage 2 Arousal. She will invite foreplay, or quickly initiate it with you. You can move smoothly through all three stages, interest, arousal and performance. This results in orgasm, hopefully for both of you, and you can hold each other, drifting off to a calm and fulfilled sleep. If however, your Interest is on level 2 and her Interest is on level 1, what do you do? You want and need sex/orgasm, but she can take or leave it. You need to be sensitively active, to switch her Interest on to level 2. The onus of responsibility is for you to touch her arousal areas in skilful foreplay, so that a level of interest of 1 can be increased, and you can move into Arousal and on into Performance. We become familiar with our partner's turn-ons; ways of being kissed, spoken to, touched in certain ways in certain places. As long as you as the male partner, take on the active seducer role, and consciously work to raise her interest level from 1 to 2, you can often be successful to engage in mutually fulfilling sex.

When there is a difference of only 1 in your interest levels your sex drives can be compatible. A difference of 2 gets much more difficult. If she is on 0 and you are on 2 there is much more of a problem. To have any chance of engaging his female partner in sex, the man has to work much harder to move her into the Interest stage and on into the Arousal Stage. Music and massage are powerful tools of influence here. Gentle nurturing touch is a very sensual experience, and releases another sexual hormone called prolactin. This switches on arousal through gentle sensual foreplay. When a woman has no apparent interest in sex, a man should take sex off the agenda and explore sensual contact. This may eventually develop into sexual intimacy. If a woman whose sexual interest is on 0, feels under expectation or pressure to have sex, it makes it more difficult for her to move off 0.

In our time of confused attitudes and beliefs about the very purpose of marriage, a marriage can last anything from six weeks to sixty years. So sex and marriage, may have a very shot or very long time involvement with each other. A couple's early falling-in-love experience, naturally makes sex a delightful and sublime experience. The falling-in-love-experience and the delights of sex combined, are a huge influence over the psychological bonding process we need to undergo as a man, to commit ourselves in marriage to a woman. In the early stage of marriage, a couple usually share and enjoy a strong erotic bond. The arrival of a child and parenthood can change this co-equal interest, temporarily or for a long time afterwards. Following the arrival of children, the pattern in many marriages, is that there gradually develops a difference in sexual interest between the partners. **Most sexual problems in marriage result from too much difference of interest.** *A married man who loves his wife, can tolerate a reasonable amount of difference between his own sexual interest and that of his partner. Too much difference of interest, becomes an emotional and psychological problem, as well as a physical one. Disappointment becomes frustration, and frustration becomes rejection, and rejection can become anger.*

If a marriage does continue over time, the general trend in the therapy room, shows that a couple have to work harder at their sexual relationship. The post feminist woman, complains about the impossible burdens of the combined roles of working as a mother/nurturer /provider. Four out of five women with dependant children now combine these roles of nurturer and provider. Many women complain that this reduces their energy and interest levels for sex. The co-equal couple of the future, will learn to co-equally share their marital roles of nurturer and provider. Each couple will decide how much time each of them will spend in the workplace, and being nurturers in the home. As men increasingly allow themselves to take on and celebrate their role as nurturing fathers, a positive spin off will be more sexual energy libido left over for women! Unless of course men start to lose interest in sex! As the couple of the future share equal responsibility for nurturing and providing, the presently overworked woman, will feel less of a drain on her sexual libido. This will have a positive influence on sexual relations between marital partners, over the long term.

Starvation of Woman: What, no Curves?

The French have a saying to describe the sexes.: "Vive la Difference!" Translated literally it means: "Long Live the Difference!" It is not a very PC idea in our post feminist world of post patriarchy. What they mean by it, is men are different from women and women are different from men. Feminism has equalised many of the cultural and social opportunities for women and men. In doing so it has sought to shrink and hide the differences.

But women are still different and
BEAUTIFUL IN THEIR DIFFERENCES
to us men.

I can only look at a woman, and see her as a man can see a woman. Today in the world of advertising, what I am shown are two kinds of Woman. Either a woman dressed as a man, with short hair and wearing a dark suit, (a man's clothes). Or if her body is exposed in any way, she is usually slim to the point of thinness; a proto anorexic. Above all, the struggle in the presentation, seems to be to conceal the parts of her body that define her as womanly; with curves, breasts and fleshiness. As a man, I see a woman's roundedness and softness as the very essence of her physical femininity. It is these qualities of curves, breasts, fleshiness, roundedness and softness that mark her out as different from me. It is her difference from me, towards which I am attracted. It is this womanly difference, which the modern media, clothes designers and perhaps women themselves, try to conceal from me. They want to show me her "straightness." She has to be hard edged, without curves and with not an ounce of extra flesh. They want to show her to me as physically more masculine. I understand that this is a fallout from the search of feminism for equality. I respect that. But hey ladies, you have that that now. Enjoy being fleshy!

I have come to the conclusion, that today as men, we are starved of Woman. As a man this is confusing and disappointing. The early feminism was in psychological terms a masculine energy. It fought epic battles to release the power of women and to assert their strength. Their struggle was for empowerment, liberation from the centuries of repressive controls we men imposed upon them. They fought for independence from men and their own autonomy. Strength, empowerment, independence, liberation. Like all movements they needed to make a strong early statement. They disguised their curves, let their breasts hang flat, shaved their heads. They threw away their "softness and femininity ". They did this deliberately to rid themselves of its historical association with weakness and gender oppression. In the 21st century, women have now achieved the progress they seek; to become heroes of their own making in an independent world of post patriarchy. They now control the world with us, and will increasingly do so in the world of the future. However, as the men of post patriarchy, we still appreciate and are attracted to the feminine as **beautiful not weak**. *Women are still beautiful to us in their difference. Roundedness, softness, fleshiness; these are physical qualities of female beauty, that arouse us to celebrate woman in all her natural charm and difference. We miss those qualities and want more of them. So let's say to the women; let yourselves curve out. Beauty is difference. Softness does not mean weakness. You have the wonderful post feminist power of Woman. You can show us your curves and still pack an equal or bigger punch than a man!*

The Lost Patriarch

Men and Spiritual Sex?

There is a great deal of confusion around about male sexuality and a man's spiritual life. We live in a highly desacralised, atheistic, western materialistic culture. The physical/material and the spiritual are considered separate. In the same way the sexual and the spiritual are kept apart. For many or most of us men, our logical rational intelligence, blocks out the mind's capacity to connect with the spiritual energy in the universe. Confronting and trying to overcome this wall of disbelief, is part of most men's essential psychological work as they journey through life. This is a great psychological malaise, and also a sexual problem for men. It has been this way for a long time in western patriarchal culture. In contrast, Indian culture and Hinduism, produced the magnificent Kama Sutra. The Kama Sutra is not merely a pictorial study of a hundred and one lovemaking positions! It is a sacred mythological text, portraying how the male female sexual relationship, can lead to a holy and transcendent mind state. In the Kama Sutra and many other human mythological stories, sex and spirit are one.

The twin sex gods, with their powerfully contrasting energies also still connect a man to his spirit. The Rampant Inner Sex God and The Love Prince are irresistible physical and spiritual forces in the male. The Rampant Inner Sex God has the sacred pagan earth energy, and was celebrated as divine in most pre-christian cultures all around the planet. His wild energy of male fertility had a natural sacredness. It was expressed in the pagan act of erotic worship. In pagan pre Christian times, orgiastic religious rituals were part of the annual cycle, connecting the Rampant Sex God to Nature and the seasons.

Whilst the Rampant Sex God is sacred earth energy, The Love Prince is heaven. He has powers of enchantment, that lift us out of ourselves into a transcendent state of mind and body. His energy is so powerful and of such a spiritual nature, it is the one that now "unbalances" our masculine psychology the most. In a godless age, where the sacred has no place in our rational mind set, we men feel ambushed by him and run away when we feel powerfully in his grip. Now, as with everything, the possibility of a new story for men is emerging. With the arrival of post patriarchy, comes the opportunity of a new sexual balance for men. Sex and the twin gods of sex are good for a man's spiritual as well as his physical and mental wellbeing. Worship your love goddess, without shame, guilt or any sense of wrongdoing. The challenge of sex and the spirit, is to find a balance between the earth energy of the Rampant Sex God, and the sublime heavenliness of the angelic Love Prince.

Male Types: "The Seeker"

We live in a time when men are alone with themselves. Their aloneness, is the natural outcome of the current fashion to avoid any form of active relationship with their **spiritual nature.** The Seeker therefore, is a man who in every sense is out of step with his time. He is totally unlike the warriors of the workplace; men driven by their desires

The Lost Patriarch

*for material achievement, status seeking and the compulsive psychology of the post capitalist Hero. In complete contrast, the Seeker has been searching for something inside himself throughout his intense young life. His search is for any opportunity to explore and discover more about what we now refer to, with a meaningless vagueness as "our spirituality". He is a dedicated, tireless self developer of his **other** side; the soulful, the imaginative, the reflective, the compassionate and the search for Love on a Grander Scale. The death of Religion in our western culture, has been replaced by the atheistic Faith of Science. Man and men we are told, are alone in a spiritually barren Universe; without any trace of or connection to a Higher Force. The Seeker is a man who's psychology, cannot and will not accept this current "Truth". A longing for the transpersonal encounter and an overpowering thirst for the spiritual high, has taken him to the loftiest and most inaccessible places in the world. He has retreated for months on end to an Indian ashram; engaged for long periods in solitary meditation in the remotest Himalayas. His studies have included the sacred secular texts of Taoism. He is a student of Lao Tzu, The Buddha, Hindusim and more esoteric Ways of Liberation. He is a compulsive reader of any book that seeks to unlock and guide the human spirit on its unending quest to connect with the sacred energy of the cosmos. His psychological journey so far through manhood, has been more difficult than that of most men. He has felt an outsider in his home country; an unwelcome visitor to his* *own homeland. A rebel to the current shibboleths of Profit, Income, Career, Equity, and Pension; women as well as other men approach him with caution and suspicion. His spiritual priorities, do not make him an ideal provider for the material wellbeing and emotional security of dependants. He is if you like narcissistic in seeking his own spiritual self fulfilment. Despite the contemporary and overwhelming Myth of Materialism, a soul-force hunger lives on in the Seeker's search for wholeness. It still burns with an undying and religious intensity in his masculine psyche.*

CHAPTER 3:
The Search for Love

Lessons in Loving

*A mother's love to her son is always **unconditional**: a post feminist woman's love to her male partner is now always **conditional.***

As an infant, as a boy, as a teenager, the male gender grows up feeding and relying on mother's unconditional love. Mother love becomes addictive. Because of it, we men carry with us, an overwhelming expectation of unconditional nurture from the opposite sex. As we grow into our teenage years, we go in search of our sexual love goddess. Our compulsive expectation to receive nurture from our female sex/love partner proclaims:

"I am a man. I deserve and expect your unconditional love." Our male love script demands of a woman that she loves us without conditions. We demand this love, both unconsciously and consciously from our girlfriends, partners and wives. This is probably the greatest emotional error that men continue to make. In a post feminist world, and in our newly emerging post patriarchy, a woman's love for a man is now totally **CONDITIONAL**. Because of this change, men somehow now have to learn to make a *quantum leap of psychological awareness, in how they relate to the opposite sex. They have to overcome their addiction to mother love and their search for alternative mother love with the love goddess. They have to learn how to overcome their compulsive expectation that the world of females, owes them an emotional living.*

A man spends the rest of his life, painfully trying to learn this lesson in loving. The various women he meets along the way of love, try to teach him this lesson in loving; with greater or lesser success. The falling-in-love-experience, is a temporary delusion of mind. When a man wakes up from it, the women he is with will be saying to him: "I am not your mother: stop expecting me to love you unconditionally like her."! He has two choices: stay and start learning the lessons in loving; or run away. Most men still prefer to run away.

The Love Programming of the Male

There comes a time in a man's life when he faces a momentous choice. What is his love destiny to be? Shall he continue to be the love taker he has been all his life? And run away when he is confronted by a woman who says: "No. My love for you is conditional, and it has to start being two-way ". Or can he face a stark reality in the psychology of love?

Can he dare to face his addiction to needing and demanding unconditional love from women?

From the first opening minutes of his life, throughout the early days, months and years of his young childhood, then on into adolescence and into manhood, all his relationships with the opposite sex, will have conspired to program him to be the addicted **taker of love.** *It all began with his safe, kind, nurturing mother. She was designed by Nature to satisfy his every baby need. Her beautiful nipples and compassionate heart, full of the milk of nurturing kindness, were always there to feed and satisfy his voracious, screaming appetite and mouth. He learned quickly how to impose his demands upon her; to always get what he needed. With her natural willingness to attend to him, he developed into an effective and highly efficient love-taking machine. If there were brothers or sisters around, he tolerated them as best he could. Deep inside, he looked upon any siblings as intruders into his special and rightful ownership of mother, and their incestuous, blissful world. One of the most difficult moments in his childhood came, when he suddenly realised that he did not have totally exclusive ownership of his mother. However, he soldiered on, using every skill and manipulative behaviour he could invent, to continue to get and take from her. Demanding, sulking, bullying, pleasing, flirting, protesting, raging; always imposing his narcissistic will upon her.*

Gradually a boy learns to make male friends. This is a different kind of "love". It involves for the first time sharing, playing together, collaboration with another human being. The pure narcissistic pleasure of love-taking remains at home with son and mother. He can return to her whenever he wants, demanding and receiving her delicious comforts and nurturing gifts. She washes for him, tidies for him, cooks for him, speaks loving words to him; is full of praise and admiration for him; adores him. In return, he stops poohing himself and learns to pee in the bathroom. He somehow accepts that she wants him to go to school, and then do a bit of homework and clean his teeth. The loving is still phenomenally one-way traffic. She provides; he takes. Then puberty happens. In many ways, this means the arrival of the best of both worlds for the by now love-demanding, love-addicted male. Mother remains there in the background, faithful, constant and providing; his stable ship of security in an ocean of change. Now he goes out in search of his love goddess. When he meets the right girl who will give herself sexually to him, he can devour and take all he wants. Empowered by the Twin Gods of Sex, he can demand, kiss, suck, lick, taste and penetrate her all he wants. He satisfies himself totally, until his one way selfish needs to pleasure and gratify himself are fulfilled. His ability to be able to give lovingly to his new love goddess, emotionally or sexually, are minimal or zero. He remains **spectacularly emotionally unintelligent.** *So far in his short male life, he has learned only how to be a love-taker. He has learned this lesson extremely well.*

He is a very good taker of love, a very poor provider of it.

Male Love and Attachment

As a general principle of our masculine psychology (not our feminine psychology in the male), a man naturally seeks to control a woman by this demanding love-taker pattern. This selfish love-taker pattern and its dominance seeking, now repels most women in their newly gained post feminist independence and search for their own self empowerment. They experience it as unacceptably controlling, and over demanding of their own finite emotional resources. The biggest complaint currently made by the post feminist women, is feeling overwhelmed by their multitasking. As an early priority of feminism, women have sought to change this egocentric love taking behaviour in men. Men have compulsively fought against this emotional initiative. This ongoing struggle, may be the biggest single factor in the current breakdown of the male female relationship. The harsh emotional reality, is that we men need to find ways of changing our attachment psychology. To begin to do that, we have to gain more understanding about how it operates inside us.

This dominance/selfishness pattern, originates from three places. Firstly it remains encoded into our genetic male programming. It emerged over million of years of primate evolution, and human natural selection. Seek dominance and control over everything, and make the world safer for yourself. We hunted and provided; and women took care of us. Secondly, we still learn it and have it reinforced, by the way our mothers care for us, as male *infants, as a boy child and as a teenager. Little boys learn at an early age to emotionally demand from and physically bully their mothers, who give in to them much more readily than to their little girls. Thirdly, many of the reinforcing dominance/control patterns of patriarchy remain with us in our culture. Male heroes in films, books, and stories all around us, still accentuate this dominance selfishness theme. They have developed over four thousand years or more, and cannot suddenly be removed in a generation or two of feminism. They continue to powerfully reinforce the genetic programming inside us: seek dominance and greater power in relationships with women; demand and take love from them. This is the stark emotional reality of our masculine attachment psychology.*

To rewrite this attachment conditioning, **men as nurturing fathers** *have a crucially influential role to play. As and when men become equal nurturers and providers, they can begin to change the love programming in their sons. In the meantime a man has to learn gradually and with great difficulty throughout his adulthood, to share emotional power in a more co-equal way with a woman. He has to discover how to give and return love to her. Achieving this momentous change, however slowly, results in enormous emotional and sexual learning for us. It opens up the possibility for us, of enjoying a relationship with a woman, that can grow and* **last over time.** *This is the great challenge in the love psychology of a man. Men are* *natural born takers of love: they are only just beginning to be natural givers of love.*

> **How do I shift from a dominance-seeking Taker to power-sharing Giver?**

This is the epic male journey in the emotional intelligence of loving.

The Love Seizure

The falling-in-love-experience, can only serve to maintain our conditioned pattern of selfishness and dominance. The falling-in-love-experience is a very intense reality. We usually get the chance to undergo it two or three times in our lives. It is a transient, transcendent, semi-delusional state of mind, body and spirit. The falling in love experience is delightful, intoxicating, sexy, romantic and ultimately artificial. It postpones us from making the journey towards our emotional manhood. It has nothing to do with beginning to learn about the process of loving. The world is now full of men, who are habitual fallers-in-love.

During the falling-in-love-experience, our senses, emotions and thoughts, are all heightened to a point of ecstatic pleasure seeking. What presses this ecstatic love button, is the attachment we temporarily make to a woman we believe, can provide it all for us. She can replace the safe, attentive, protective mother we have enjoyed taking love from all our life; and she will give us all the erotic pleasures of the love goddess that our twin sex gods demand of her. Our absolute priority in life, is still to seek out achievements and compete well enough with other males. To find our heroic path and commit ourselves to it. This is the priority for us, so that we can grow the male ego. We have not yet learned in any genuine way, to understand how to give love to others. This still does not seem to be important to us. The world seems to work well enough with us doing our own thing. At work, at home, in our fantasy making, on the sports field, out with the lads. We are still fundamentally being driven by heroism, machismo and selflove.

In the old world of patriarchy this worked well enough. The old world was the pre-feminist world. The world when the principles of patriarchy still reigned. The world where becoming and living the life of a man was, emotionally unbalanced and psychologically one dimensional. Tune into the masculine force and live its selfishness to the limit. Women were expected to be happy and content providing and giving the love; we practiced the taking.

From Love Taker to Love Provider

Our moment of love destiny is fast arriving. It arrives when the woman we believed could always be our love goddess and substitute mother, finally becomes unbalanced by our relentless taking and demanding from her. She will now have her own career which challenges and demands from her. She may now also have a young child or children to care for. After years of our demanding, protesting, needing and taking, she finally screams at us in despair; "I cannot live with you any longer. You have to change or we will have to separate." We are shocked, disbelieving that she can mean this. We have reached the compelling moment of disillusionment in the male psychology of love and attachment. The wheel of love and attachment has turned.

For the first time in our lives we are being confronted with a fundamentally different reality. A vastly different life comes into view; the male love taker has to learn how to grow into the male love provider. The boy/man who has only known how to function as the 90%-100% taker, has quickly to evolve somehow into the man 50%-50% giver-taker. There are many reasons for this compelling psycho-cultural change: post feminism, post patriarchy, motherhood, fatherhood, co-equality, work-life balance, the new family system. Whatever the combination of reasons, the shock to our male psychology runs deep and is profound. At this point in a relationship many of us run away. We turn the woman with whom we have been living, into an un-nurturing cold bitch. We abandon her before she can abandon us. We find another woman, who is still appears willing to play the 90%-100% game of giver taker.

Some of us stay. Slowly we find the emotional courage to face the hardest and most frightening challenge of our manhood. We study the art of loving. Men have a deep emotional ignorance of the essentials of the art of loving. We have to be educated, starting with the basics.

The Basic Arts of Loving for Men: 5 Principles

The art of loving is based on five principles.

> **Kindness   Attention**
> **Generosity**
> **Empathy   Forgiveness**

Men have to become students of the art of loving, at a very basic level. Our instructor is usually the love goddess with whom we have decided to stay, after she has threatened to abandon us. The wonderful thing is that as we learn slowly about loving, life comes alive for us in a new way. Gradually, bit by bit we become freer from our life long male addiction to demand, take and receive from others. We begin to tune into a different kind of loving; to give, to pay attention to and be kind to others. Developing our kindness, generosity and giving of attention, becomes a pleasure for us. Those close to us, learn to receive it with delight. This pleases us. Their being pleased, gives us pleasure. A whole new "circle of love" grows and lights up around us. Our male psychology undergoes a gradual but radical shift from self gratifying love taker, to loving others. As we learn the five principles of loving, we begin to see the new emotional possibilities that surround us. They are everywhere; in our relationship with our partner, our children, our friends, our work colleagues, our community and ultimately with the planet itself.

As our love re-programming proceeds, we slowly escape the addiction we have developed throughout infancy, childhood, our teenage years and on into the early years of adulthood and partnership. If we stay and undergo this love re-programming, guided by our love goddess, we are becoming men of the future. We become liberated from a way of feeling and thinking that belonged to the patriarchal past; our individual past and the past of our culture. Evolving a new balance between self love and loving others, between being the love taker and the love giver, opens up a future of change for ourselves, our culture and ultimately our species and planet. This psychological process of how to become a loving man, is at the centre of our male liberation.

A man has to recognise that this kind of loving is like a wheel. Each one of us is attached to the wheel. For it to keep on turning, each one of us must apply some energy and momentum to it, to maintain its forward momentum.

Kindness *is the first and most basic aspect of loving. To connect with his kindness, a man needs to open up to the flow of love that instinctively sits in his heart. It is literally like a great spiritual river, that once released will flow with an infinite ease. Sadly, most of the male's conditioning influence, (especially in childhood and adolescence), insists that this kindness is a weakness, a softness that is anti male, and too feminising. He learns at a very young age to block that river's flow. Finding ways to change this patriarchal psychology of the male, is one of the greatest challenges that faces us, in our search for a new post patriarchal identity* *for the manhood. Tough guys don't do tenderness; or do they? Heroes don't do nurture, or do they? Kindness is weakness, or is it?*

Attention *is the next aspect of loving the male needs to learn. Obsessed and over driven by his own addiction to bringing love into himself, his under developed emotional intelligence, needs to learn how to pay attention to the needs of another person. He needs to temporarily forget, his lifelong habit of always paying attention to his own needs, (physical, emotional, sexual). He must learn somehow to begin to give his focus and concern, to the other person and persons around him in his life. The post feminist woman, demands that she see him and pay attention to her. Just by sitting, looking and studying another person, a man grows this aspect of his loving psychology. Gradually he is able to escape for longer periods from the bubble of his own narcissism. He comes to feel safer outside of it, and that he will not disappear if thinking about and giving attention to others.*

Generosity *is the next aspect of his loving which a man needs to learn how to grow. In contrast to sport, business, buying, demanding, bullying, borrowing, taking, stealing; generosity is about giving away. Generosity is about letting someone else have, what you probably want. With a female partner this is typically about generosity with time, or money, your/their own space. With children, it is about being generous with your attention giving and being child focussed. The self gratifying male ago, finds this aspect of* *loving perhaps the most difficult to learn. Searching for his own gratification, challenges and achievements, a man learns to be mean. The post feminist woman accuses him most of this and he is still often described as an absent partner and father.*

Empathy: *this is a loving action that requires emotional imagination. How do you imagine how the other person, (partner, child, friend, colleague) might be feeling at any one moment? To do this, a man needs to learn how to think and feel outside of himself. He has to learn how to receive the other person's energy and needs, with focus and concern. This means he has to learn how to tune into his feminine psychology, which naturally receives and responds to another person with openness and sensitivity. Empathy is a more psychologically advanced stage of loving, and develops spontaneously from the living practise of the previous three aspects of loving: kindness, attention and generosity. When a man can be empathic in a relationship, he is getting clever with his emotional intelligence. He understands how a person feels the way they do, and he is gaining insight into the behaviour that they are showing.*

Forgiveness *presents the biggest challenge to the male of the species, in his learning of the five aspects of loving. This is because from a very early age he has been conditioned to "stand up for himself". In standing up for himself, he has learned to impose his will upon the world. To make it as much as possible, the way he wishes it to be. When something goes wrong, because somebody disappoints him* *in this wish, he gets irritated, cross, angry, even violent with his emotions and fists. A mummy who is not immediately there, when he wants her to be there. A girlfriend who does not want to have sex when, he wants to have sex. A wife who did not cook supper when she promised she would, because she herself was late home from her work. Forgiveness challenges a man's loving psychology, at its most fundamental level. Learning to accept the changing world more as it is. Learning to overcome your disappointment and resentment at others, who are unable to fulfil all your selfish expectations; and learning to forgive them.*

Less than 10

There was a very popular film in the 1970's call "10". The title described the woman in the film, who scored 10 (maximum), in all departments. She had the looks of a Love Goddess. She made love like an angel. She possessed a soft, warm, nurturing personality, and meticulously attended to her partner's needs. In so many ways she was any man's dream female. She was the fantasy woman come true, standing before him in her beautiful bare flesh. Here in the 21st century, 10 still lives on. Walking down any city high street or watching the loveliest looking film star in the cinema, a man can still be seduced by the promise of a 10. From numerous bill board adverts, 10 stares down at us, with her seductive all promising allure. Beautiful sex, beautiful glamour, and a nurturing female who indulges all or most of our male selfishness. Almost wherever he looks *now, a man still cannot escape the marketing and media presentation of a 10.*

When we meet our "dream' woman " the statistic 10 emerges from our male psyche. 10 represents perfection. The perfect, ideal woman. 10 out of 10 is the best you can get. When she can score 10 in a number of departments, we begin to think of partnership, marriage, fatherhood and families. It is when we are in the 10 stage of the falling in love experience, that we are most likely to take on a commitment to one woman. It is only by staying with the perfect woman long enough, that we begin to witness her perfection, (her 10 qualities) fading before our eyes. Some days her looks are less than perfect; or she is not always able to be available to look after us. Or she is irritable or bad tempered, or she is not always available for sex. Slowly, the perfect ideal woman of 10 begins to show her imperfections to us. Gradually, day by day, we emerge out of the-falling-in-love seizure that has overtaken us. We come to see the woman as she more genuinely is. Not through the fantasy lens of a 10, but with a reality lens, that allows us to view her imperfections as well her many real qualities.

The conflict in relationships really starts to take off at this point. It is when the psychological task of learning to live with a real person, begins. In a very true sense, the woman we fall in love with, is not a real person at all. She is a trigger for something stored up inside us men: powerful images of the Love Goddess and the perfect Mother. A particular woman, somehow switches on these images, that then come alive and beam onto her for 6 or 9 months or a even a year. Then they fade a little, and we can start to see the real woman and person in front of us. Usually that is when the trouble starts.

Despite all the enormous changes occurring in our post patriarchal culture, romantic myths still tell us stories of gorgeous yielding maidens swept off their feet, by powerful seductive princes, who then live together for a happily ever after lifetime. This is the Fairy Tale whose powerful influence we still grow up under. Maybe we need to emerge beyond the fairy tale.

Psychologically speaking, we men have very little insight into the process we call, "falling in love." Before finding it, we know it is out there, or supposed to be. When we do find the experience with that special woman, although anticipated, it still comes as a shock and surprise. We experience it (her), as a form of soul intoxication. A drugging of the mind, body and spirit, all at once and to an astonishingly intense degree. A kind of seizure of body, mind and spirit occurs, in which ongoing reality is suspended. Our male psychology experiences a degree of longing that can only be satisfied by one thing; time with and within the other person, the woman. There is no lasting satisfaction. The desire keeps coming, it is endless. We become a different kind of man, initiated at last into the mythical world of "Romance". We understand the stories of Love in a new way. Love poems connect immediately and deeply with our emotions. We want to write them ourselves. Pop songs overwhelm us.

Their lyrics and musical language, cut through to our very core, with an infectious emotional power.

What we do not realise is that the other person, the woman, is not the drug. She (the love goddess we find), only switches on a latent time bomb of entrancement, already implanted within us and waiting to explode. It has been encoded into our male psyche, by the evolution of our male gender, over aeons of time. All of us men, carry around within us an inner image, an archetype of the Love Goddess. When released by a relationship with the appropriate woman, the archetypal image explodes, releasing a drug like ecstasy which once experienced, changes us for ever. From then onwards, we have all become love goddess addicts, romance junkies, for the rest of our lives. Once tasted, the erotic longing for the Love Goddess is searched for, throughout the rest of our lives. Being with the Love Goddess is a very special place when we are "in love." Our union with her is magical, transcendent. In love with her, we imagine and believe we can be all things. In some psychological sense, we cannot really understand, there is truth in this. She is the Muse, the inspiration that moves us on to greater and better things. Without her, we cannot find the deeper things in ourselves. Like the male hero with whom we can identify, she too releases a new power in us. With her we can go on to better and stronger things. Through loving and being in love with her, we can know and express, a potential we could not know otherwise. This is all the upside of the falling-in-love experience.

Stephen Duke

Male Types: "Superior Action Man"

We are all familiar with the action man. Whatever sport or piece of DIY we do or have done, he has done it first: and better, more often, faster, on foreign soil, or solo. Of course, he himself usually no longer does it, and with a polite put down, implies that he used to do it, but has now moved on to more manly pastimes. If we are in training to run a half marathon, he has already run three full marathons. If we like body boarding he is into windsurfing. He constantly seeks out the higher challenge, the new ultimate test to push himself even harder, further, longer and more dangerously. Action man is the compulsive sensation seeker and would be Boys Own Hero. His heroes row the Atlantic solo, march to the North pole, sail solo around the globe, open the batting for England or play outside half for them at rugby.

Superior Action Man is the ultimate male competitor. His ego thirsts compulsively for competition. Victory and conquest are the life blood of his self image. He is driven by his hormones and competitive ego to run, cycle, swim, climb, explore and test his prowess against others, to the point of physical and mental exhaustion and beyond. He is a seriously committed devotee of all water sports: sailing, water ski-ing, scuba diving and wind surfing are all part of his action panorama. He has at least two ski-ing holidays a year, testing his courage and prowess off piste with a reckless abandon for his physical safety. Above all action man is compelled to **do** it.

Occupationally, action man will often thrive as an entrepreneur, successfully starting up his own small business. Frequently however he finds himself working as a teacher, having initially been attracted to the profession by its long holidays and week ends, freeing him to celebrate his many sporting interests. Soon however, the classroom becomes a dark prison for him, a place of unending routine, predictability and frustration. This drives him to escape into the hills and the wilds with even more passion, and drive his senses to further extremes of sensation seeking.

Action man is also a compulsive Mr. Fix It. For him the glass is always half full, and this optimism enables him to take on any job within and outside the home. He decorates, builds walls, fixes broken washing machines, mends cookers, and is a dedicated car mechanic. These practical homemaking talents, (as much his sexual gifts), can make him very attractive to a particular kind of women. Sexually however, action man is renowned as a short stayer. His sexual performance and lack of sexual control are usually unfulfilling to his female partners. He is a prime candidate for premature ejaculation problems in later life. Action man is primed for conquest rather that co-operation, individual performance rather than team work, going solo rather than enjoying togetherness.

The psychological life crisis arrives for action man, when a shattering life event happens to him. Grief, illness, divorce, redundancy, loss or any combination of these, overwhelms his tireless optimism and life practicality. He is suddenly forced to look inward. His seriously neglected introverted side, now demands that he at last give it his full attention. He becomes depressed, feels useless, his life has no meaning. His fragile male ego, organised around the immediate material world and the senses, languishes forlorn and hopeless. He is compelled to feel and reflect, consider and be still. He must begin to learn how to utilise the richness of his inner resources. To engage with his imagination, intuition, and connect with his hitherto unexpressed spirituality. If his life crisis is fully lived as a creative crisis, action man will emerge from it a much changed person.

CHAPTER 4:
"Forming Families"

Post Patriarchy and The New Lifestyle of Families

Put at its simplest, a family is any human psychological and biological unit, that has one of the four parent-child relationships: mother/son, mother/daughter, father/son, father/daughter. It can be made up of any combination of these. When or if as a man, you decide one day to form a family with your female partner, before you jump straight in, there is a lot to think about! To last over time, it will probably need to be a very different type of family unit, from the one in which you yourself grew up. The way women now want to live their family lives, has changed fundamentally over the last twenty years; and it will continue to change even more in the next twenty. This has enormous implications for you as a man.

These changes will be:

WOMEN WILL WORK MORE AS ACHIEVERS AND PROVIDERS. MEN WILL BE MORE IN THE HOME, AND BECOME MORE INVOLVED AS NURTURERS TO CHILDREN. THIS WILL BRING HUGE CHANGES IN *CHILDREN/ PARENT BONDING*

*Times are not just changing for men; they have already changed! The problem is most men cannot allow themselves to fully **see** the changes. Men are still consciously and unconsciously resisting the changes, that women have already made and continue to make, in the male female relationship in families. Women have changed themselves forever. Their emotional, sexual, work and family behaviours have totally transformed in the last thirty years. There are also some roles they now refuse to play, and these are often the roles we men still want and expect then to play!*

Women as mothers still take the greater responsibility for childcare; but they also have their own agenda for achievement and their careers. Four out of five women with school age dependant children, now have careers. Half of mothers with very young children, aged under five, are now in work.

Today's women are simultaneously

ACHIEVERS-PROVIDERS-NURTURERS

Women are also having children later in life. Delaying the role of mother/nurturer, allows them to achieve more, earlier. They can establish themselves well in a profession, before deciding whether and when to become a mother. The attitude of female workers has also changed. Women are growing more ambitious as they become key players in the world of work, contributing to major company successes. The impact of the female boss is considerably more powerful than ever before. The pressure for women to achieve, drives them to work harder and for longer. They want to prove themselves to their female peers, their mothers, their male counterparts, but most of all to themselves.

Women **and** *men are both taking on multiple family and work roles. This role combining and role exchange is at the emotional heart of the new psychology of the post patriarchal family. Men have always happily played the first two roles of achiever and provider. This was the fundamental hero stuff for a man in patriarchy. Now a third role is opening up for them. Men are now doing more of the care responsibilities. According to research by the Equal Opportunities Commission, a surprising 36% of couples say that the man is the* **main carer***. Polls also show that more and more fathers feel they are missing out emotionally, due to their* **lack of intimate contact time** *with their children. Men as active father/nurturers are coming alive in a new way. So the changes in family life in post patriarchy, are fundamental ones. As women increasingly set their own achievement agenda, they become providers for the family in their own right. For some men this seems to enable them to "liberate" their nurturing qualities.*

THE NEW BALANCE

The Emotional Ecology of Families

To help you get a sense of how families develop, try thinking of you and partner, and any child or children you have together **as a psychological system.**

> **A Family system is a network of intimate relationships, each with its own particular psychological agenda that is constantly changing and growing. Husband/Wife- Father/Son- Mother/Daughter- Mother/Son-Father/Daughter. Each has its own special themes and patterns and dynamics.**

The emotional system of the family forms when you and your partner get together and make a commitment. You and she are the centre of that system or circle of love. Becoming a parent is like entering another emotional universe. You may be one of those men who looked forward to it, and planned the whole thing. You may be a man to whom it just happened, like life just happens! Either way, it is an emotional, physical and financial life change; that keeps going on. You spend the rest of your life celebrating and sometimes struggling, with its psychological consequences.

A Quantum Shift

No man knows what it is going to be like; nothing can prepare you for it. When you have your first child, the system of two that you were, suddenly becomes a three. You only add one, but you go from one pair to three pairs: the couple, father/child, mother/child. A big shift; a quantum shift of family psychology. For the rest of your time together, until your child or children leave home, you will be negotiating hard for solo time alone, or time together as a couple, or getting the balance of attention giving to your child or being a family circle. For the first year, your child's needs will take absolute priority. As a man, this means needing to struggle with opposite feelings: the joy and exhilaration of becoming a parent, and feelings of emotional displacement and being overlooked physically/ sexually by your partner. Before you became a three, you had your partner/wife as your exclusive companion. She was companion, love goddess and nurturing mother combined in one. She was there to meet your selfish male needs, more or less whenever you wanted them met. As a constant companion with hobbies, entertainment and friends, she was also sexually available more or less whenever you wanted her. Your intimacy was satisfying for you as a two.

We are a species that gets most of what we need physically, emotionally, sexually, psychologically **in a two**. *So, when the child suddenly arrives, you have become* **a three**. *This sounds simple. But it is profoundly important. In families always look for the twos and the threes. Inevitably then, there is rivalry for time, energy, intimacy between the twos. You have grown into a fundamentally different family system, overnight! The shock is profound, and you need time to assimilate the developing psychological consequences of it. The psychology of your attachment to your partner, is* *fundamentally different to your attachment psychology with your child. As you lose some of the intimacy of time with your partner, so you begin to gain a growing attachment and intimacy with your child. As you learn slowly, to accustom yourself to the change, the new emotional family system that you have become, grows into a new balance. Your positive attachment to your new child, your father love, helps you tolerate your loss of time and intimacy with your partner. However, not all the time. You enjoyed your intimacy time with your partner so much, that you committed yourself to her. That hungry desire for her, does not suddenly stop overnight, because you have become a father! A lot of men struggle to find a new balance within the triangle. This is especially the case now. In the newly emerging post patriarchal family, the arrival of their child, confronts them with learning how to combine the new male roles of* **achiever-provider-nurturer**. *To do this, begin to learn to be as honest as you can with yourself and your partner, about how you feel. Don't hide the feelings you have of being left out or wanting solo time, of feeling neglected or frustrated. Tell your partner if you want more intimacy, be open with yourself and her. And importantly, allow yourself time to grow into the new emotional family system you have become; from 2 to 3. It cannot be done overnight.*

We men can allow ourselves now to be more **the nurturing father**. *In patriarchy men experienced a genetic and social programming to be achievers/heroes/providers. This only expressed our masculine, heroic psychology. It* repressed our nurturing feminine psychology. Now in post patriarchy, women have their own liberated script to live as Achievers/Heroines/Providers. For the family of three and four, to operate practically and emotionally, we men must now willingly take on and enjoy greater emotional responsibilities as nurturers. We must embrace this emerging role as a key aspect of our emerging male liberation. This means having to overcome our anxiety that such a role in any way threatens loss to our male ego and personal power. Rather the opposite. We have to actively embrace and explore for ourselves within our post patriarchal families, the new balance of hero and homemaker, provider and nurturer. We must recognise it as the huge opportunity it offers, to release our repressed feminine psychology, alongside our masculine heroic energy and allow the New Balance to integrate inside us. This means greater empowerment as a man. Becoming a nurturing father, does not mean giving up and abandoning the active, masculine pursuits that give us a rounded psychological balance. Men must learn to welcome it as an opportunity to become more evolved, in their roles within the post-patriarchal family unit.

The family of the future will become a totally balanced triangle of Nurture-Achievement-Provision. Father and mother, man and woman, sharing equal time for nurture of their child/ren, with an equal shared commitment to the world of achievement and work.

Central to this personal and cultural change in the emotional ecology of families, is the concept of **the co-equal couple.** The co-equal couple of the future, will have learnt to skilfully pass between them and to share, the roles of achiever and nurturer, provider and homemaker. Women's ongoing liberation for self empowerment and achievement outside the home and family, provides an equal opportunity for male liberation. That is, for men to express the dormant nurturing qualities in our masculine psychology, previously so repressed by the institutions and conditioning influences of patriarchy. This is the way forward for men and the New Balance.

There remains though for most of us men, a core conflict for us in our manhood psychology. The time we spend at home nurturing, is time not spent on the hero quest, (however we choose to pursue it in its 21st century form.)

The next century is an evolutionary experiment in the changing balance, between our hero psychology (masculine) and our nurturing psychology (feminine).

A fundamental aspect of this experiment, is for a man to find an emotional balance within a new form of family, and his search for achievement at work. The evolutionary pressure is now strongly active on men and the male psyche. How many generations will they need to achieve that change, only time will tell.

From 3 to 4

The first step from being a couple, to becoming a family with a child, is a quantum leap. The next step is also a huge one. Moving from three to four is almost as big a step in family making, as moving from two to three. In having a second child and fourth family member, you grow from being a system of three twos, to a system of six twos! If you have a son and daughter these are: father son, mother son, father daughter, mother daughter, brother sister, partner/partner. Quite a lot of relationship psychology!

But what really takes off in this new system you have become, is the number of triangles. Before there was only one triangle, mother father child. Now there are almost too many to count! Triangles breed rivalry and emotional stress. We are a species that likes to do most of our serious intimacy living in pair bonds. We can get and give most of our needs for contact, closeness and intimacy in a pair bond of some type. Mother and baby, father and son, man and woman, friend and friend, brother and brother, sister and sister. These are relationships that have a good chance of satisfying the needs we have for pleasure, fun, security, sex, creativity and companionship. They provide the intimacy we crave from infancy to old age.

Triangles are a different system altogether. In a triangle somebody is always feeling left out, or actually is being left out. One of the three is always feeling they can't get in, and they have to try harder to push themselves in. The rivalries and needs are so strong, that balance and stability in family *triangles is difficult to maintain. This triangular psychology causes much of the emotional conflict in families. The human family triangle is inherently rivalrous, competitive, and tends to be emotionally unstable. We experience it as stressful. If you are the father in the middle of two demanding children, you have to work harder to spread your focus and attention equally to each one. If you are the husband in the triangle of three, (mother, father and child), it is often difficult for either adult to get what they want. If an argument brews up around bedtime, between your partner and your son, (when you are exhausted after a day at work), you have to take on the role of peacemaker. There is no escape in family triangles, and they are all around you, most of the time!*

Tricks for emotional survival in family triangles

Here are a few tricks to help your emotional survival in families. If you find your mood suddenly changes, from up to down or tension rises inside you:

1. Look around you and search out what emotional family triangle might have entangled you. In many families the father/man, is still routinely asked to take on the role of final authority figure within the home. This can be to defuse the conflict between your partner and a child, or the conflict between child and child. This is okay up to a point. But sometimes it might be best to pass back to your partner the role of hardman. Over time playing the role of the ultimate authority can create fear between you and a child, and goes against the role of the nurturing father. It can create a barrier for closeness, softness and intimacy, between you and your children.

2. The most effective solution for all of these problem triangles is to go **one on one**. In a family of three, break up and form a two and one. Then negotiate your way through the problem. In a family of four, break up and form two parent child pairs. The effect of this is always to neutralise the triangle stress. You will not banish the emotional rivalry and conflict forever, but you will defuse it immediately. Then there is more time for reflection and discussion. The family system can get back more into balance.

Remember: the principle is twos are inherently more stable, triangles more inherently unstable.

Always go back to the two. And if there is anytime left over after all this, use it for yourself!!

Couples and Family "Scripts"

A family forms emotionally, when a man and a woman experience the love seizure and then go on to commit to each other. When a couple forms, their two individual psychological stories and their family scripts or emotional stories combine as well. The woman to whom you love and commit yourself brings with her, her own family's script and emotional story; and the important characters who live

The Lost Patriarch

within it. Her mother, her father, brothers or sisters come with her. Has there been a recent divorce in her family or a bereavement? All of these and a multitude of other events go to create her family story or script.

You also have your own emotional script from your family of origin. Your feelings about your father, mother, brothers, sisters. Also the values and beliefs about the lifestyle you want to live, are importantly derived from the family in which you have grown up. How important is work, play, ambition, sex, music, the garden, children, fatherhood? You hold powerful beliefs about all of these things, some of which you are aware, some not so aware.

You and you partner co-create together a new couple script, made of pieces of each of the two family's scripts you bring to your relationship. This can be a gentle intermingling of family stories and beliefs. Or it can become a violent collision! A common and almost inevitable area of conflict, is what a man as partner and father, should do and be. Your female partner has grown up watching a man from the earlier generation of men. Although a post feminist woman, she may still actually be quite attracted to some of the male behaviour she witnessed from her father: strong, protective, a man who takes most of the responsibility for providing and offering her security, materially and emotionally. She may consciously believe that she is happier with a more contemporary man; a domestic god, a co-equal partner. **Unconsciously however, she may well be more emotionally attached to images of manhood from**

her family script and the role of her own traditional patriarchal father in it. Confused and confusing? It is. It is the consequence of living in these times of great changes in gender psychology. Everything is in the melting pot.

There is another factor that makes the psychological processes in the male female relationship during our time of post patriarchy, confusing and unstable. You as a man/partner, will bring your own post feminist, post patriarchal ideas and beliefs, about what a woman is and should be. You will have bring your expectations about how she should behave, into the partnership/marriage. Ideas and beliefs are one thing; <u>emotions</u> go deeper and can ambush you. We men have to begin by recognising that Nature still programmes us, to want to go out and be hero-hunter-providers. Many of us will have grown up with mothers who **were** always there for us and our fathers, when we all came home. This is the family script that we grew up with, and at some deep level we would have liked to continue. We still want at some deep level, to have "our woman" sitting at home for us when we return. This programming however, locks her in a psychological cage from which she has escaped, with the key of feminism. This will leave us unconsciously confused, insecure, uncertain.

The new couple have to begin by recognising, that it is now all change for men and woman, and that the change is only really just beginning. It has a long way to go. How fast can we achieve it? We men have to begin by opening up to the confusing and contradictory emotions and attitudes *we have about power, equality, family roles, mothering, fathering, providing, freedom and independence within marriage or partnership.*

The post patriarchal, co-equal couple are improvising and experimenting with who and what they can be. They are making it up together; no roles or rules are set in stone. The script of the couple in the new post patriarchy, is being radically re-written. The gender patterns of thousands of years of living and lifestyle are being overturned and broken up. In the generations to come, a new mythology for manhood will emerge and the couple will be living out their lives to new couple scripts.

Marriage as we have known it in patriarchy is falling apart. Breakdown and divorce rates are now 1 in 2. Caught as we are, somewhere in the transition from patriarchy into post patriarchy, marriage and family making is at the centre of the cultural re-invention process, of which we are all individually a part. To live together and stay together, a man and a woman are having to learn a great new trick: how to juggle between them the roles of achiever/provider and homemaker/nurturer. They are having to learn how to become a co-equal juggling act, catching, carrying and sharing the emotional responsibilities of childcare and the challenges of career and the workplace. This is what feminism liberated in a woman; the right to be a self achieving woman first and a mother second. This is what the post feminist female insists she has a right to be.

THE CO-EQUAL COUPLE

Co-Equal Attachment

The quantum shift in our gender psychology and the development of more co-equal couples, means men are becoming more consistently active over time as nurturing fathers. They spend more time hands on, learning the child centred nurturing skills of being a parent father. There is a profound psychological consequence that will inevitably flow from this. More and more they will become **co equal attachment figures**, *for their children.*

This is in contrast to patriarchy, where fathers were so much absent provider figures. In vastly increasing numbers, (as well as still being hero/providers), we men are spending more time within the home and with our new born infants and young children. As we do this, we are becoming as important emotionally and psychologically to them as their mothers, in making the world a safe and secure place. Consequently, we are become intensely and powerfully bonded to them and them with us, from the outset of their young lives. Gradually as men grow their role as nurturers as well as providers, the intensity of bonding with their children will become on the same level as that of mothers. **We become co-equal attachment parents to our children.** This is a new and fundamental shift in the psychology of post patriarchal parenting. It is a key aspect of the New Balance that lies ahead of men and their changing psychology of the future.

Fathers and Sons

Fathers and sons love and oppose each other, seek and enjoy closeness with each other and also struggle to find it. There is always that masculine essence to their relationship. A man can understand this best, when he has lived both roles. He needs to have been a son to his father, and then become a father to his own son. The feelings of rivalry a father can feel for a son, are all in contrast to the positive and protective feelings of warmth he can also feel towards his son. A father's emotional loyalties to his male heir, can pull him this way and that. He stares at his newborn son as he holds him in his arms, hypnotised by his tiny and vulnerable male child. He feels his instincts and duty to both protect and induct his son into the masculine ways of the world. A father's love for his son is complex, ambiguous, and full of contradictions; truly masculine.

Stephen Duke

When a man becomes father to a son, he will be surprised how his own experience of being a son to his own father, begins to come to the surface again. His son's birth will release some of the memory of the relationship with his own father. The psychology of this is interesting. Suddenly he is no longer just a son to his own dead or living father, the younger less powerful male. He is now the responsible father, the stronger more powerful one. How he experienced his own fathering, pleasant or unpleasant, empowering or abusive, nurturing or neglectful, shapes much of his own nurturing approach as a father. There is long chain of nurturing love, conflict and competition that characterises fathers and sons, continuing through patriarchy over thousands of generations. We can think of the father son relationship as a vast seam of male memory and experience, formed and shaped over thousands of generations of time. It is deep, rich, intense, powerful, archetypal and mysterious to women. The relationship between fathers and sons still remains at the centre of the fabric of our post patriarchal culture.

The future suggests a father who is more actively nurturing of his son, in a hands on way from birth, through infancy and on into childhood. In contrast to the patriarchal father who was more absent and therefore emotionally distant, the father son relationship of the future, suggests more intimacy, closeness and attachment. Fathers and sons will still need to do their boys stuff together; they will in fact have more time for their "masculine" pursuits of sport, learning etc. I also see a father son relationship that will be slowly changing over time in coming post patriarchy.

We all know from our role as the son, that things go wrong in the father son relationship. Sons are compelled in their search for their own emerging identity, to challenge and ignore father's authority. This is when the ugly issues of authority, control and discipline raise their head. Modern child psychology shows us that if the father gives the son much more praise, warmth and respect than criticism, they will always enjoy closeness. This closeness will enable the son to follow the father's advice when he feels he needs to provide it. Most of the time this can be true. Sometimes it will fail. Fathers and sons will come into conflict. This is inevitable and someone has to win. In a functional family, it cannot be the son.

Stephen Duke

Father-in Law and her family script

A CLASH OF FAMILY SCRIPTS

The family script into which you marry, can be confusing with regards to images of manhood. Many men describe their struggle with someone from "her family", and the emotional script which their partner brings into the marriage from her family.

The father-in-law/son-in-law relationship can sometimes be an area of psychological collision. A man, when he takes on the new role of son-in-law, will almost inevitably intermingle his feelings about his own father, with his father-in-law. This includes a desire to be recognised, respected, approved and accepted by his new "father." In this sense a man cannot have too much good fathering. He may not have received enough love and approval from his own father. His father may have left after a divorce, or he may have been the emotionally frozen patriarch, who could never be emotionally demonstrative. He was the father unable to be close to his son's needs for kindness, tenderness and approval. This type of son-in-law is especially hungry for good fathering. He looks to his new substitute father, his father-in-law, to provide him with some of what he still needs as a son.

So the relationship can take on a great deal of psychological importance in the new family script, created by the new couple. A man will also want the relationship with his father-in-law to be a success, to please and win the approval of his new wife. Fathers and daughters (his wife), more typically are close, warmly attached and in personal harmony together. Fathers are almost universally pleased with their daughters when they are born. A father always wants the best for his "little princess", and this includes the type of man she chooses to marry. All of this is in the family script, and sets the psychological tone of the father-in-law/son-in-law relationship. Expectations of dependability, achievement, reliability and sound performance are brought to the son-in-law role from her family script. This is one of the true burdens of manhood; is my husband as good as my father?! Is that guy good enough for my daughter?

Can you turn out to be his/their type of man? How far do your images of manhood fit his/theirs? How far are you playing out the role in the way you do, because you believe he (father-in-law) wants you to?

One final thought on this subject of father-in-law and son-in law. A daughter has three psychological options when she chooses you as her partner/husband. Either you are the kind of man she thinks her father would like and approve of; or she chooses because you are different from him and challenge his values and beliefs. Or you are a combination of both! The good guy role is the easier one to play. You are chosen because you repeat a lot of his stuff about manhood, which she liked about her father and wants from you. But this good guy role, is getting harder and harder to play, as each generation of males is faced with increasingly radical change about what manhood and being a partner is all about. It is getting harder and harder to "fit" what her father was about. The bad guy role, (being chosen by her to be different from him), is of course tough. You are chosen to be a companion rebel against him, by her. For example he was an accountant who made it onto the board as a financial director, and sent his children to public school. You on the other hand are a musician, struggling to get a regular work and your first mortgage at the age of thirty-five. Look at the cartoon again! The third option, a mixture of both the same and different as him, gives you a chance of success with him.

He starts out suspicious of you but likes what you remind him of about himself. So you have something to build on; and he can learn to accept your differences and come to respect you for them. Good luck.

Male Myths of Manhood and Family Scripts

I have described some aspects of the psychology of the family script, and the way it directly and powerfully affects the way a man views himself as a man. In the family in which we grow up, this is usually about following the story of manhood given to us by our father. How much do we want to follow a manhood path that repeats or challenges that of our father? Fathers and sons can get into a lot of trouble with each other over this. Myths, traditional stories of manhood, build up around a number of male themes. These can include: "making it" in the world, earning money, how a man should behave in his marriage, achieving in sport, being disciplined and setting discipline, friendship, showing and feeling emotions, spirituality and religions. The thing is you can either repeat your family's script, or you can try to correct it.

For example, now many young men are deciding to live differently from their father. This is part of the cultural change process of which each one of us is now a part. Therefore you are then correcting or rewriting the manhood family script. You are putting it right as you see it. Perhaps you feel your father worried too much about his career, to the detriment of his being available to you, his son. So you decide to live your life in a more relaxed way, searching for a different work-life balance. You work harder at being more available and therefore emotionally closer to your son. So the story of the family script evolves and changes from generation to generation. You have corrected an over distant relationship between father/son. What kind of fathering do you think your son will give to his son?

Over countless generations of patriarchy, the patterns of behaviour and psychological "myths" have built up in the collective family script, about the **nature of manhood.** *The family script is an all powerful set of beliefs, held largely unconsciously in the minds of family members. For example, nineteenth century beliefs still remain powerful in the family scripts of many families today. They continue to determine much about how fathers and sons relate to each other. Much of the continuing and future struggle for fathers and sons, is to let go of much of this psychological heritage. In the nineteenth century, fathers became more and more physically remote from their sons. Closeness and tenderness between father and son was viewed as weakness; emotional distance between them as typical and being cut off from emotions as a strength. Fathers were authoritarian, dominating, disguised their feelings, and put work, moneymaking and religion before all else.*

In contrast to the last two hundred years, men now have a great opportunity to bring emotional healing and a new intimacy to the father and son relationship. Gradually we are getting better at understanding the closeness, contact and intimacy issues that are important for us. This is one of the key aims of the new balance we are searching for in our manhood. The father of today and the future, is trying to be emotionally attached to his son in a new way. All of this movement of change, reflects a gradual reversion of the **myths of masculinity**, taken from our wider culture, and played out in the scripts of families. We create our families and their scripts, which mirror and express the broader beliefs from our culture. As the contemporary father seeks a new balance in his masculinity by tuning into his nurturing softer side, the family myth of the father who is a work obsessed and emotionally frozen patriarch, slowly dies away. It is being replaced by a very different image of what makes a good father.

How is Domestic Democracy Possible?

More and more, women of the future will want to live with, and will expect a domestic democracy within the home. This means a shared, co-equal balance in lifestyle and roles within and outside the home. In order for this to begin to be possible between any couple, the first principle is:

CONSTANT DIALOGUE: about who does what, for whom, why and when?

To be able to begin to stand up to the challenges of domestic democracy, men have to recognise one fundamental and uncomfortable truth. The uncertainty and resentment at the changes in women, lies very deep in us. The comfortable fit of patriarchy around our masculine psychology, is being taken away layer by layer. Many men still resent and are angry about what they see as the changes initiated by women, and then enforced upon them unwillingly. Unconsciously many men are marrying a woman, to try and ensnare her back into the patriarchal prison of a dominating marriage with traditional power roles. This does not last. Women leave after a lot of mutual unhappiness and conflict.

A genuine crisis of manhood identity is ongoing in the roles of men at the home and at work. Men need to confront themselves with their uncomfortable feelings about this; anxiety, confusion, self doubt, uncertainty, resentment, anger, loss.

This emotional and psychological work has to be done by each man. Only then can a new system of post patriarchy, and the future of men in the home and family, be co-invented. If men allow themselves to start from where they genuinely are, then they can become active in the process of reinventing themselves. Patriarchy is passing; as it leaves us we feel a sense of loss and uncertainty. At the same time, a new future of possibilities is coming into view.

A home and the family who live in it, is a complex physical, psychological and financial system. More and more, a man is expected by a woman, to share and live the role of domestic god alongside her domestic goddess. Patriarchy let men go off to achieve and compete with each other in the workplace, and to provide through success and that competition. They returned home to a nurturing domestic goddess, who prepared warm welcoming meals,

The Lost Patriarch

provided regular sex, and in the meantime did all of the house cleaning and nappy changing, while he occasionally changed a few plugs! (Perhaps an ideal but remember the story at the beginning of the book about this couple. It is a very contemporary post patriarchal tale of marital disappointment and failure.) Post Patriarchy, presents an entirely different balance and framework for the gender roles within family life.

Married women or women in family partnerships, now go out to work, where they compete with themselves for success and achievement. Then they come home tired and worn out like their male partners, after a hard day's toil. Like them, they then need to be taken care of and restored to balance. This is often a time of a **clash of needs,** *with either the man, or woman, or both, not feeling sufficiently well taken care of by the other. This is when CONSTANT DIALOGUE comes to the rescue. By talking and listening to each other, the priority of each other's neediness can be recognized, and then a plan put into practice. This is domestic democracy in action.*

The principle for men that makes this possible, is the recognition of the new co-equality between couples. In Post Patriarchy, a woman's commitment to her work outside the home, has become a major life priority. Like men have always done, women now take up their own challenges outside the home. Like men, they thrive on getting to grips with them and overcoming them. Women are now finding themselves, as men have always done through competition, commitment and challenge. The post-feminist woman is on her own course of self-exploration, self-discovery and self-actualization. Since her liberation, she sees and confronts many of the same questions as men, in her own search for happiness.

In this confused difficult time for men, women continue to set much of the agenda for living. Men have to take serious time out, and begin to reflect on what all this means for them and the fundamental issue of their manhood identity.

MEN NEED TO UNDERSTAND QUESTIONS FOR THEIR POST FEMINIST PARTNER

What is my challenge?
How much does it dominate my life?
What is success and how much of it do I need?
How much money do I need to earn?
What is the right work-life balance for me?
When is it right for me to become a mother, if at all?
Do I need a male partner or to get married?
Will I find a man who understands my need for co-equal partnership?
Can I find a man who understands and will share in domestic democracy?

They need to focus their personal reflection on the four crucial areas, of work, family, marriage and identity.

Half of all marriages now fail, and many of the other half become a confused struggle for identity, power and equality. As we will see, innocent children are caught up in the battle for power, identity and equality between their two parents. Children will always suffer enormous emotional damage, when their parents separate and families breakup.

Love, Competition and the 21st Century Couple.

In the recent Hollywood made movie called "Big Daddy", the **nurturing "mother" is the father***. The man/hero character learns slowly and happily how to nurture a young boy, whom he meets and then legally adopts. In doing so, this man slowly heals his own emotionally cut-off relationship with his own father. The man's father is a highly successful and ruthless lawyer. An absent high achieving father, he was never at home enough if at all, to father his son emotionally in any way. He always put career and achievement before all else. Because of this, their father-son attachment was weak and insecure, and the son dis-identified with his father. He is left with disillusionment and anger, that he is compelled to heal and overcome. He wanders around with no ambition or clear identity until he finds a way to become a good father. So the son grows up by becoming a very different kind of nurturing, emotionally present father to the boy he learns to love and then adopts. In doing so he re-writes his own highly dysfunctional father son script.*

While learning to love his young adopted son, the man has also fallen in love with a dedicated career woman who is a highly successful lawyer! For much of the movie, her emotional dilemma is whether she can find time or the energy for any relationship, let alone any form of stepmotherhood for the man's adopted son. At the final adoption hearing, the adopting father happily states to the court, that his lawyer girlfriend earns enough money for all of them. She can provide financial security and he can provide the emotional security and nurture for the new family they wish now to form.

This story is a very post patriarchal tale, in which the traditional patriarchal gender roles of parenting have been completely inverted. The woman is totally dedicated (over dedicated?)to her career and work ambitions. She has the relentless, selfish drive needed for career success and the financial rewards that come with it. She is driven, by her own masculine heroine psychology and her compelling need for achievement. The man in complete contrast, has no achievement script, but is a loving, nurturing and emotionally generous father to his adopted son. He is the love center of the family circle/triangle the three of them create together. He is the caring emotional heart of their family system. The homemaker. In this post feminist story, we see the masculine energy fully unleashed in the female. That is her energy to compete, to achieve and succeed in her career, at all costs to her emotional life in relationships, is what drives her life. She is rescued from this one-sidedness by the loving man, whose nurturing emotions rescue her back into a better balance. Together they create the balanced post patriarchal couple who work out their emotional system in their own way.

Powergirl, Post Feminism and Machismo

Nowadays, the story of Big Daddy and its characters are not inaccurate fantasy fictions. The world of business and corporate life, is full of women in their late twenties and early thirties whose life priority is achievement. Powergirl is a post feminist phenomenon. (See the cartoon of her again). She is dedicated to achievement and her career, and therefore highly successful in her professional path. Women now achieve in whatever field of human activity they choose, from medicine to bricklaying to sailing solo faster than men around the world. Work-life balance can more problematic. Powergirl complains she is often unhappy and alone in her emotional life with men. Powergirl cannot and will not play the supportive role of home making partner/wife. To many men, her success is a dangerous threat to his potential success. The fragile tower of the male ego, its machismo and a man's own inner hero, shake. Consequently many men in their current mood, will tend to avoid pairing off with powergirl in a long lasting loving relationship.

Girls on top can find the rewards of their success, increasingly difficult to share with any man of their choice. The liberated, career successful woman, faces a post feminist quest which she has invented for herself. It has three key themes in the narrative:

How much of myself can be rewarded through work?
How much through partnership with a man/relationship?
How much through motherhood and family life?

Only by finding her own answers, can she discover what is the balance of work-life, in which she can feel complete and fulfilled. Research shows that she is still trying to find this balance in the emerging context of post patriarchy.

The movie Big Daddy shows a man, who has rejected his own hero psychology, for the exclusive role of nurturer/homemaker. He is portrayed as contented and fulfilled, by staying at home with his adopted son. His male ego appears to have no problems with his woman partner, earning all the money and being the sole provider for the family. For most men this is not the way it works. But change is happening, and needs to carry on happening. We men are facing momentous changes in patterns of work, nurture, life sharing and work-life balance. Most of us are only beginning to be aware of what the change is and why it is happening. Many of us are still fighting back stubbornly and often destructively with our wounded machismo and patriarchal beliefs about manhood. Or else we are running away from the battle of change, to another relationship. So often we face the same issues there with another woman.

The man living with the post-feminist woman, needs to develop his awareness of her as both someone he loves, and as someone with whom he feels rivalrous. The individual needs of the co-equal couple of the future, will in some ways often be in rivalry and competition with each other. There are two very contrasting mind sets associated with lovers and rivals. In emotional terms, it means that a man can be feeling tender and adoring towards a woman, and very soon afterwards tense, resentful and angry towards her. And it will still be the same woman with whom he is living. Mothers give to their sons, with unrelentingly kindness and generosity throughout their boy childhood. Men bring that egocentric love taking pattern to their female partner, who more and more as a post feminist resents and rejects it. Women want and expect men to love with an equal give and take. Women now expect and want as much from men, as men want from them.

In the marriage of the future there will be fewer and fewer women who "love too much." When they see and experience men giving to them, they will continue to give. This is Love in its 21st century guise. Remember that the five qualities of loving, kindness, generosity, attention, empathy and forgiveness, do not come spontaneously to the male. They are aspects of the Feminine: women are more in touch with those qualities of loving. For men they come harder, because the egocentric heroic/masculine wants to squeeze them out. The 21st century couple, both want to express their independent, goal seeking, and masculine side.

To make this possible women understand they need more support from their man. If he is unable or unwilling to give it, they will withdraw their giving side, and an increasingly angry stalemate develops. Unless change happens in the relationship one or other walks away.

The post patriarchal couple often struggle to maintain balance and harmony, because there may be **too much masculine energy in the relationship.** *In psychological terms there is too much outgoing achieving energy, insufficiently balanced by the nurturing feminine. How the couple of the future, work out their passionate rivalry for achievement outside the home, whilst managing childcare and homemaking within it, is the big issue.*

Increasingly there is rivalry for many men with their female partner, about **achievement outside the home**. *There is more of this to come. It is the way forward for post patriarchy. The world of the future will be inhabited by couples, who have to find their own unique solution to this issue. They will have to find for themselves, the balance of achievement and success, with nurture and homemaking. Men can accept success for their female partner, but get edgy if they feel they are giving their own away to help their female partner achieve her success! There is a profound and disturbing fear for men, that emerges with the success of women. Many men fear that they are being replaced in the world of work by women. They also fear the growing success of women, because it threatens to take away the most important masculine role of patriarchy: a men as the*

Hero/Provider. **This tension of roles is at the center of the emerging crisis in the identity of manhood.** *We need to examine this to understand it more deeply.*

Sex, Achievement and Male Machismo

With a decline in the power of the hero role, male machismo and sexuality can be affected. Machismo is part of the most primal energy of the male. It is our elemental force, evolved over millions of years. It enables us to compete with Nature and the forces of survival. It is symbolized by the bull, the stag, the horn, the phallus, the sword: all images of domination or male power. Challenges or competition of any kind will trigger it. The Sex Gods flourish with our machismo. Both the Sex Gods and male machismo feel under threat in the post patriarchal world. Male sexuality and machismo are two deep parallel rivers, of the same primal force than flow constantly inside a man. Men whose heroic ego identity cannot be successfully released at work and in the provider role, often become depressed and then can lose interest in sex.

Sexuality and achievement go together in way we need to understand psychologically. There is scene in the English movie called "The Full Monty" about five guys who are trying to become male strippers, after losing their normal jobs through redundancy. One of them, is lying in bed with his wife who wants sex. He turns away, temporarily unable to get an erection. He has become psychologically impotent, as his sense of masculine identity languishes in his non-achievement at work. Ego, machismo, masculinity, work, achievement, sexual performance, heroism, identity; all of these core issues are involved in the currently changing themes in the meaning of manhood.

There is a core difficulty at present in the male female relationship, that revolves around these themes. A man feels sexual love towards a woman. He seeks emotional attachment to her and sexual intimacy with her. In the same loving, intimate attachment, her independence seeking, her achievements and success in the world, can fill men with emotional and sexual anxiety. Men do feel threatened and psychically endangered by the new independence and liberation of women. Male machismo, the core primal masculinity of the male, seems to need to fight back against her, in a darkly instinctive attempt to regain dominance over her. This can only be a retrograde, backward looking instinctive reaction, that is connected to the more primitive heritage of the male psyche. What the male and female of the species needs to do, is learn co-operation, harmony and balance in the new co-equal couple relationship. This has to be based on a mutual understanding of the need for a man and woman, each to fulfill their living potential.

Increasingly, powergirl may out achieve her male partner in career terms. In the future she may well earn more money, gain as much or more career recognition and status. Her ability to compete, to achieve, to go out there and take it all on and be successful at it her own goals, does not have to be a dangerous threat to manhood, masculinity and its own goals. Her "masculinity" and our masculinity *need not be seen as rivals, in direct competition with each other. They need to both be seen as working for the greater good of the relationship. More money, more success, more satisfaction and ultimately more balance for the couple's relationship.*

Men must search and discover a changing balance between their heroic ego identity, their desire for achievement, their sexual machismo; and their feminine, nurturing qualities as homemakers and carers of children. This is the living experience of the emerging psychology of a male liberation which lies ahead of men. Patriarchy repressed men. It kept them one sided and unbalanced. Post patriarchy is an evolutionary step forward that will allow men to become more complete. The responsibility for change lies firmly with them, to make the family of the future operate as a stable and enduring emotional unit. They need to find a new evolutionary balance between their instincts to provide and their capacity to nurture.

Stephen Duke

How do I become a Domestic God?

DOMESTIC GOD

The picture above shows the domestic god and goddess at home. How do men evolve into domestic gods alongside their domestic goddesses? What are the qualities men need to discover in themselves. What do they need to liberate in themselves?

To begin with: whatever she is prepared to do, he will have to be prepared in principle, to do as well. This means every domestic task from cleaning the loo, to hanging out the washing, getting up for the 4 o'clock baby feed, cooking and childcare etc etc etc. Collaboration and task sharing become a priority. For example drying one child's hair whilst she washes the other child's in the bath, hoovering, ironing, supervising homework, supervising bedtimes and stories, shopping for provisions, collecting the kids from school, buying the kids school clothes.

Perhaps doing all of these things on your day off, while she goes off to a conference at work. Are you shocked? Appalled? If so, this is your patriarchal programming, prompting you to react with disdain against the truly liberating role of the domestic god. Ready to put the book down? You have to realize that you can only be elevated to the lofty status of domestic god, by fulfilling a huge range of routine but highly significant domestic activities. Each task, each action (they must not be labeled chores because that degrades them), scores important points towards graduation. You know you have joined your domestic goddess as a domestic god of equal status, when you can participate in these routine daily events, and celebrate them within your home with her and your children. As a domestic god you enjoy and celebrate them, because they help you feel more and more intimately attached to your partner and children. They center you emotionally in the heart of the family circle you create, when your new family forms. They connect you to your home and partner and children in a way you have not experienced before, and did not think you could experience in this way.

The question of cooking should never have become a problem for the male gender. Men all over the world have loved to cook and celebrate the products of their gardens and Nature, in the kitchen. The notion that a woman has been enslaved to the stove by her male partner, can be done away with at a stroke. You can do all of the cooking or most of it. Or one day she cooks, the next you do. Or the routine is organized, around the coming home from work routine, that you have agreed from your respective work schedules.

The 10 Minutes that Save the Marriage

There is a potential emotional flashpoint, even between the perfectly tuned in domestic god and goddess. They need to learn how to honour their routine to overcome it. When one or other returns from work, or both return together, they share the 10 minutes that saves the marriage or relationship. The essential idea of this is to find a way to be mutually nurturing, after a demanding day at work. The couple sit and form a bubble around themselves and talk; drink tea, coffee, eat a biscuit, ice cream anything that gives them pleasure. They then report and discuss the day's events together. Having been apart for eight or ten hours, the priority is to re-connect and share intimacy for a period of time. Whatever they decide to drink or eat they experience contact and tune back into each other and regain intimacy. They must tune themselves back into each other's energy waves. There are three advantages to gained by the domestic god and goddess when they do this.

1. They are put back into close contact with each other, de-role from their achievement script, and switch off their work-achiever emotions and mind set.
2. A new level of home communication is now possible. The dialogues that are essential for a domestic democracy

The Lost Patriarch

to happen, can begin afresh each day. Domestic tasks and plans can be made, in which home time is to be shared together.

3. Most important of all, each can feel attended to by the other. Remember that we always crave attention and are hungry for nurturing. This is especially the case for both individuals in the couple, after a day in the workplace. If each of them gets a little, and gives a little as soon as they come home, then their needs for nurturing will be satisfied to some extent.

Another great benefit of this couple re-connection time, is that it staves off resentments that can build up, through feeling neglected by the other person. People who feel neglected, tend to sullenly withdraw from each other. They feel hurt that they are not getting the attention they deserve and crave. If these negative feelings go on, they build up. Later on there can be an explosion of resentment and mutual recrimination. Accusations are thrown against the other person that they are selfish and unloving. The ten minutes of tuning in and re-connection time, can go a long way in preventing this from happening.

During the ten minutes that saves the marriage, it may become clear that one of you needs to "go to the cave" to rest and withdraw from the frenzied world. She may have had a particularly tough day with her work. With low energy and needing time for recovery and to restore, you can give that to her. Tomorrow, it may be you who needs the time out, and to go solo in the home for a period of recovery. All this can be successfully negotiated; but it has to begin with the ten minutes that saves the marriage/relationship.

Learning how to negotiate and form a team with your domestic goddess, over the most routine domestic matters, is much of the skill of the domestic god. Teamwork is essential, and has to be based around a daily mantra or saying for the couple. You can use this with each other when negotiating. Here are some suggestions:

"THIS IS NOT EQUAL"
"MY TIME AND YOUR TIME ARE N0T THE SAME"
"THIS IS NOT GOOD"

When one or other of you feels that what you are being asked to do, makes the sharing of tasks unequal, you use your mantra to convey your displeasure. Or you can use the mantra, if you feel the other one is not doing enough of what you think they should be doing, to make the teamwork equal. Calling out the mantra such as "this is not equal" will focus the two of you into a dialogue, and usually results in a positive response from your partner. Cleaning the house, shopping for food and provisions, hoovering, ironing and other traditional areas of "womanly" homemaking, are still thought to be in opposition to his machismo by the patriarchal male. The post patriarchal man who is trying to become a domestic god, may hear a scornful self mocking voice, whispering quietly inside his head. This voice is full *of disdain and contempt for such homemaking tasks. To his father, they were considered unmanly feminine tasks involved with service and submission. A patriarchal man has a deep underlying anxiety about his machismo being shamed if he carries them out on a regular basis. The real reason for this lies in the subconscious of the love-taking male that all or most men still are. He relished the one way domestic service that mother and his family of origin homes used to provide. It is this mother-son conditioning that tries to perpetuate the pattern of woman as giver and man as taker.*

This mindset belonged to patriarchy. The post patriarchal domestic god, has to learn to happily re-invent himself within the co-equal couple relationship and create a new type of home.

The domestic god celebrates teamwork and mutual homemaking, with a new gender mindset of co-equal co-operation with his female partner. They share in co-equal homemaking and house management. The psychological challenge to the post patriarchal male is: am I secure enough in my emerging manhood identity, to be able to re-invent myself in the role of a domestic god? His patriarchal script, learned from his father, and reinforced by films, television, books, the male peer group and wider culture, (quite a heady mix), can still block his desire to re-invent himself as the domestic god. The liberated man however, can see his machismo for what it is: something that belongs outside the home and shown sometimes to other men; on the field of games or used occasionally to strengthen his search for achievement. He is the newly balanced man; equally comfortable in his manhood roles on the rugby field or wearing his pinny in the home! His manhood psychology is equally relaxed, when tuned into his masculine side out in the world of achievement and work, or when tuned into his feminine side within the home.

He is as tough as he needs to be
and
as soft as he wants to be.

There is another emotional and physical bonus, to a man who can learn to comfortably play the role of domestic god. You will notice that the picture is quite playfully sexy. The hoover is there, representing all the tasks that need to be shared in the home. However the couple are partly undressed. The implication is that teamwork and collaboration between the domestic god and goddess promotes fuller intimacy, and is usually good for their sex life! Your partnership with her, your teamwork with her, washing cleaning, ironing, cooking, shopping, keeps both of your energy levels more equal. Intimacy is enjoyed doing these things together and as a direct consequence sex and lovemaking become more regularly possible. The woman is not full of resentment at his neglect of her, while she works at two full time jobs; one of them unpaid in the home. By re-inventing yourself as the domestic god, you can reign supreme in the sexual heaven of your home, in the blissful company of your sexy domestic love goddess. The home has become for you, not just a place to return to and escape from. It is a haven that is the centre of your life, lived in and celebrated alongside her and all your family.

Why do Dragons look like Mother-in-Laws?

A VISIT FROM THE MOTHER-IN-LAW

To understand the complex web of relationships that form a family, we also have to discuss the relationship between yourself and the mother of the woman you decided to love. There are a great many jokes made about mother-

in- laws. This is often to hide anxiety and anger about her. Sometimes the psychological fit is very comfortable. However on many occasions, the son-in-law can become harried and haunted by the mother of the woman he has married. This is such a universal phenomenon that it needs further exploration, from a reflective psychological viewpoint on the forming family.

To begin with, you do not choose the mother of the woman you happen to fall in love with, and whom you eventually marry. (I have written a lengthy section on Falling in Love; and the key thing to remember is that you are driven by your non-rational psychology. That is to say you only have very limited control, or none at all, over the choice with whom it happens.) So you fall in love and marry someone, driven by your non-rational side about which you have little understanding, and over which you have even less control. Along with that woman, to whom you were attracted without really knowing why, comes an older woman, her mother, as part of the physical and emotional "baggage." The woman you love, loves another woman, with an intense childlike attachment. They are bonded together like ice and fire.

To that older woman, your mother-in-law, the woman you love, will always be to some extent "my little daughter". This is human nature. It is also at the centre of family psychology. You believed, you were climbing into a twosome, just you and the woman you love, your wife/ partner. Pretty soon (sometimes even before the marriage has taken place), you realise you are also married into an intense, emotional triangle of at times deadly rivalries.

Human triangles as we have seen are complicated emotional systems. Your naïve male fantasy was that it was just you and your wife. You thought her childlike feelings towards her mother were something of the past; unimportant compared to your feelings and the newly found love and commitment to each other. Soon slowly, bit-by-bit, a different truth begins to dawn on you. Triangles are complicated because, instead of it being just you and your wife (one pair), there are three pairs: you/your wife, your wife/her mother, your mother-in-law/you. Human triangles have to work very hard to be calm and stable. More often than not they are emotionally competitive and struggle to stay balanced.

How does all this play itself out in your everyday, married life drama of you, your wife and your mother-in-law? How does she become the dragon we all know about and fear? The first thing you will find yourself getting caught up in is, The Family Script . You marry into a family script. Think of the family script as the epic drama of your partner's family story, played out over generations of time. It includes all the characters and people in her extended family. It has great themes like; how a man should behave or not behave, what a woman must do, what makes a good or bad career, what makes a good father, and much else besides. (Remember too, that your family has its own family script that your wife marries into: this is what makes her mother-in-law, your mother, a friend or a dragon to your wife!) Quite unintentionally then, you have married into this great ongoing epic family drama, which now wants to include you as another character actor in its story. One of the main scriptwriters of the story, is, you guessed it, your mother-in-law. The potential for conflict between you and her, is dependant on one principle: how willing are you to follow their family script as it is written, or how much do you feel the need to challenge it, in order to be yourself?

Here is an example of going out of your way to fit into the script. I recently met a man aged thirty five, who had been a professional actor all his adult life male life. He had been very happy and fulfilled as a creative man, with his own strong sense of identity in this occupation. He had just married a very beautiful young woman, herself an actress. Her mother, (his new mother in law), made it very clear that his profession did not fit the role a man and husband was expected to play in their family script. In their family script, men were bankers, lawyers, doctors, city brokers, teachers; above all regular providers! They could do almost anything but be actors. In their family story, a man was expected to be a reliable, regularly employed, provider and financial protector. From the moment he first met his new mother-in-law to be, this future son-in-law received a great deal of his new mother-in-law's disapproval, of his unsuitable and unmanly profession. Gradually, inexorably, inevitably, this had such an emotionally powerful impact on her new son-in-law, that he surrendered his loyalty to the

The Lost Patriarch

acting profession within six months of marriage; and took up horticultural design. Very different from playing Hamlet.

This is a fairly extreme example of doing your best to fit into the new family script. It is not untypical. Generally speaking, at the outset of a marriage, a man will at least try and play along with the mother-law's- new script for him. This is to avoid causing too much distress and anxiety to the woman he loves, his wife. If the relationship between his wife and her mother is good, (which it generally is), she herself will hold many of the beliefs and values from her family's script. To carry on winning the love and approval of his wife, a man will therefore consciously and unconsciously, play along with the script. There is however, a real danger in the longer term, that by seeking to avoid conflict, a man may feel he is having to compromise too much. Even to the extent that he may begin to feel he is losing some of his own unique individual identity. Wife and mother in law, (mother and daughter), make a very powerful psychological alliance. Ultimately only you as a man can write your own life script, within you and your wife's marriage. No one else can write for you and her as the new couple; not even the mother-in- law.

When (in order to hang on to his identity), a man starts challenging and rebelling against some aspect of the family script into which he has married, this may well cause anxiety and concern to his wife and partner. She is in the middle of the triangle between her mother and him. The strong emotional attachment between her and her mother, pulls her loyalties one and then another; away from her mother towards you and then back again towards her mother, away from you. As I have explained elsewhere in the book, mother/daughter is one of the four archetypal human relationships between parent and child. Because there are two women involved, this is the most mysterious to us men, of the four. Fathers and sons we intimately know about. Mothers and sons we have intimate experience of as well. Fathers and daughters many of us will also have direct experience of, even though our "little girl" is female, and from the more mysterious opposite sex. Although you may well have had the opportunity to observe mother and daughter before, within your own family, this may not have been the case. Even if you do have a mother and sister, how well do you understand the emotional intimacy of their attachment? If you have a sister, you may without knowing it, assume your mother-in-law and your new wife, will follow all the same emotional rules as they do. They may not. You may not have a sister. Therefore, when you marry, this will be the first time you become emotionally entangled with a mother and daughter bond.

When you first met your wife, she will have been in the period of her life, when she was most independent of her mother. Nowadays when they leave home, most women establish their own careers. They may have a succession of relationships with men, and fully live the liberated life; professionally, sexually, emotionally. When you meet a woman and she marries you, this starts to

The Lost Patriarch

change. It's as if the family script comes more alive again in her. Whatever you and she may have done as boyfriend and girlfriend; wandered the globe, lived as vegetarians, fought as eco-warriors, produced films, started your own porn business, written poetry and novels together, your marriage, commitment and parenthood will always bring about huge changes. This is especially so when children and motherhood arrive.

There is one simple way to begin to escape the family script. If you feel tyrannised by it (and mother-in-law), learn to write your own new script together, **as a couple**. To do this, you will have to do quite a lot of talking about the respective baggage you bring, from your own families. This is not as easy as it sounds. As I described earlier, the family script goes deep. Your partner's family-of-origin script will have written into it, a good deal about who your wife is and should later become. It wants to include you in that story, as a new character. The same goes for your family script, about you. It wants to include her in its story. Somewhere, somehow, you have to start doing it your way, and write your own new story as a couple, together.

To begin to do this, you need to understand a few more things about family scripts, mothers and daughters. All relationships have to work out their own rules of **distance and closeness.** One key question to ask and answer is: how much closeness, how much distance is there, between your wife and her mother, your mother in law? Distance and closeness is both emotional and geographical. Remember, *when you met your wife, she was almost certainly at her most independent, and therefore distant from her mother. This is almost certain to change. There are two reasons for this. Firstly, if and when she becomes a mother, as she probably will, she and her mother will get closer again. The bond of motherhood is a powerful one between women, and nearly always brings mothers and daughter closer again. A daughter wins important recognition and love from her parents. This is especially so of her mother, because by becoming a mother she provides her mother with a grandchild. They will understand each other in a new way and live with a new closeness; and they will need each other in a new way.*

The second factor which often tends to bring mothers and daughters closer together, is the simple and inevitable process of both getting older. As your mother-in-law ages, she may well become more dependant on and demanding of, her daughter's time and attention. The rules in families of mother and daughter relationships, often tend to be that daughters gradually take more care of their mothers as they age. In many families, the influence of mother-in-laws on their daughters, remains a powerfully active one. Because of this, mother-in-laws will very often be some kind of rival to their son-in-law; for the time and emotions of the woman they both need and love. Neediness becomes competitive. There is one final thought on husbands, wives and mother in laws. Despite all the complex emotions and psychology I have discussed, your new mother in law may look upon you as the perfect partner for her daughter. It does happen!

Her Father; and you as Son-in-Law.

If it is true that in the psychology of marriage, men still look for alternative mothering, it can also be true that women look for alternative fathering from men. How much does a woman's father intrude into a couple's marriage, psychologically and practically? How does it make the relationship more or less difficult between them? What problem areas can it throw up?

Her father has certainly been the most powerful influence over what a woman likes and dislikes, wants and does not want, from a man. In that sense, a man has to recognise that he is always being matched up to his partner's father in some way. This is both a conscious process of which she is aware, and sometimes unconsciously unaware. A woman can compare her new male partner in any number of ways: does he protect her and the children as well as her father did? Does he provide for them as well as her father did? Is he as good at working on the home? Does he give as much attention and love to her as her own father did to her mother? Or is he much better at doing all of those things?

Being constantly measured up like this can be a huge strain on the marriage and relationship. Her father lived in his time and had his advantages and disadvantages. The world is a different place now for men. Men now live in a post patriarchy, and finding their manhood is a different process in this time. Can women stop themselves comparing their partner to their father? There is a lot of psychological business, to be sorted out between you and your partner, and you need time to unravel it together.

Couples Exercise: *Do this together in a quiet space. Ask each other these questions and write down the answers, so that when you get into conflict you can refer back to them.*

Man: How am I like your father?
Woman: You are like my father because......................
Man: How am I different from your father?
Woman: You are different from my father because...................
Man: What do you like about me that's like your father?
Woman: I like the way you are like my father when............................
Man: What do you like about me that's different from you father?
Woman: I like the way you are different from my father..............

I think you will learn some interesting things from this exercise and it will go some way to unravelling the family script, and its continuing influence on your marriage and relationship.

The End of Marriage

One third of modern couples, who have children together, will not marry. And the figures are rising all the time. These couples prefer to try and live together as a man and a woman. They make the huge commitment of

The Lost Patriarch

becoming parents together, but something makes them retreat from the ultimate commitment of a marriage.

The men in these unmarried relationships argue that if they love a woman, they no longer need in the changed post feminist culture of today, to prove it to them by marrying them. Others say that marriage belongs to a different time and age, called patriarchy. And they understand that we live now in a different world of post patriarchy. Others say that divorce rates prove that marriage does not work for a life time of happiness together, so why do it? They also argue that the law no longer penalises couples and parents who are not married.

Many men say that because of the divorce laws, men and fathers get a raw deal emotionally and financially when families break up. They say that nowadays, their children will not be shamed amongst their friends, for having parents who are not married. Many men no longer have any religious faith, that impels them to marry a woman with whom they live or have a child. These men (and women) are independent and are freethinking, and are not afraid to challenge the values and traditions of their parents. They are prepared to re-write the family script on marriage. The message they are giving to their parents is clear: "we no longer believe that marriage is necessary, to make a family."

So one third of couples, who have children will not marry. One in two of those couples who **do marry**, split up within the first five years. Many of those divorced men, then go on to re marry. The divorce rate of second marriages *is even higher than first marriages! It is profoundly clear from all this evidence that marriage is no longer operating successfully as an emotional and legal arrangement. A happily married couple who have been living together for more than ten years is today, the rare exception. For some reason though men keep on trying it. Perhaps men believe in marriage more than women now do. The latest research suggests that two out of three marriages are ended by unhappy women. Many women complain in their greater financial and emotional independence, that they begin to feel trapped in marriage. They complain of feeling frustrated and angry, living with a man who does not recognise the need to change. And so they leave.*

This crisis in marriage, is a direct outcome of the ongoing crisis in the male female relationship of post patriarchy.

Marriage is one of the main stages, upon which the wider drama of change between men and women, is now being acted out. As we go further into post patriarchy, we may be witnessing the **terminal decline of marriage**. *It seems increasingly unlikely that in the future, a man or a woman will be fulfilled, by sharing their life with just one partner. Men and women, will have too many opportunities for their personal development, to want to stay throughout a life time of personal growth and change, with one person. The increasingly vibrant, exciting opportunities for self development and self fulfilment, that now exist for men* *and women, means that they simply outgrow each other. Marriage in its old Christian patriarchal form, by definition implied a lifetime of commitment and faithfulness. This is in opposition to the post feminist human potential movement, in which both men and women increasingly find themselves. It seems highly likely that women in particular will more and more see marriage as a dis-empowering restriction to their personal growth, in the long term. So commitment by becoming partners, without marriage, offers the new co-equal couple, a crucially new balance between them. It recognises mutual opportunities for a man and a woman, and for the process of personal change that is common to both of them; for as long as it works for them.*

What happens to a man and father when they break up, is not a process we understand or properly recognise for its profound impact.

Male Types: "Mr. Adverts"

*Mr. Adverts is the quintessential "man of the moment". More than most of us males, he is up with the trends; indeed he lives for and through them. Whether in the style of his clothes, the magazines he reads, the music he listens to, the television programmes he watches, or the car he drives; he is cool. He works in an advertising agency. His manhood seeks its primary expression in the procreation of the materialist myth: namely, if men work hard for the acquisition of the goods that lure us, true happiness can be acquired. His genuinely creative and artistic skills, are corrupted on a daily basis for the purpose of **selling**. He is an art whore.*

Stephen Duke

Fast cars, garden equipment, condoms, low fat yoghurts, holidays in the sun, plasma televisions, household insurance, pensions, sportswear, lager; he can turn his seductive talents for presentation, towards any item or service the businesses have currently developed for our consumption. A prostitute to his genuine talents for painting, design, architecture and sculpture, he left art school seduced by the rewards of advertising and his narcissism. Any sense of self betrayal is well hidden from his self adoring ego. His self esteem is high, because he survives in an industry that is hyper-competitive, and he is victorious often enough over other men who are his constant rivals.

In the longer term there is a psychological problem for him: for how long can he remain a creature of the superficial and soulless? For how long can his deep inner integrity, his drive to genuine self knowledge and personal growth, remain distracted by the world of the ephemeral and materialist illusion? Sooner, or later he must address his inner condition. He will become wearier and wearier of the anxiety that he must look younger than his age; that he must keep ahead of the other trendy, talented younger guys in the office. The process of aging, both physical and psychological, will eventually catch up with him. His crisis of identity will come later in mid-life than for most men. He will tire of the misuse of his imagination and soul, to set artificial trends in the slick world of selling. Eventually, through a midlife crisis brought on by redundancy, illness, bereavement or divorce, he will confront the artificiality of his existence head on. Then at last, he will be able to begin to break free of the enslavement of self and spirit, that the bonds of his chosen career superficially encased him within. He will be able to feel, think, and imagine more genuinely: to live and find himself, rather than pose and role play in the world of manufactured trendiness For Mr. Adverts the word fashion, will take on a new meaning to him: he will fashion himself in Life.

CHAPTER 5:
"Families Breaking Up"

Here are so opening thoughts about families breaking up.

In emotional terms for anyone, there is no such thing as an "easy" divorce
Divorce=Man in Life Transition

When mummies and daddies stop loving each other,
kids start hurting!
Sons get angry; daughters get anxious and sad
For men as fathers, it has to get worse before it gets better
A man has to recover from two emotional losses;
the loss of an intimate partnership
the breakup of the family circle
Men's emotional pain is greater than that of women,
because most children, stay more of the time with most mothers
Men's pain is getting worse when families breakup,
because men are closer to their children than ever before

**Men tend to rush into other committed relationships
before properly healed.**

The THREE stages of DIVORCE

Stage 1 Breakup.

Shock, rage, fear, confusion, life disorientation, loss of confidence, loss of sex drive, loss of appetite, sleep deprivation (lasts 2-4 weeks)

Stage 2. Seperation

Isolation, mourning, mood swings, angry outbursts, overeating, drinking, low moods, sleep disturbance, depression, anger, loss of interests, thoughts of self harm, search for new sexual partners (last 3-9 months)

Stage 3 Recovery

Regaining emotional stability, beginning of homemaking, recreation of a new family circle, gradual recovery of life interest, increasing sense of independence, sex drive returns, better sleep patterns, return of interest in female relationships, return of social confidence, mourning continues (6-12 months)

The Shock of Breakup

When marriages end and families begin to breakup, a major catastrophe occurs in the life of a man. As a direct consequence, he undergoes an overwhelming range of emotional experiences; shock, fear, anxiety, pain, loss and anger. (This is true, even when he is the one who has broken up the family, and may also have gone straight to another woman.) It is a disastrous emotional and psychological event, for which he can never be prepared. He has enjoyed a continuous, deep, emotional and sexual **attachment** to a woman, for years; this suddenly comes to an end, and somewhere in his male psyche it feels like the disaster it is.

Despite the period of conflict that almost always precedes the actual moment of breakup, a man undergoes a **shock of abandonment** that resonates to the deepest levels of his masculine psychology. In the first few hours and days of being left, (or leaving), he regresses to his emotional childhood. He re-experiences emotions he felt at a very young age. Typically this is around two or three years old, when he was first learning to gain some physical and emotional independence from his mother. So for the first few hours and days, he really feels like he has been abandoned by his mother. His loses temporarily, his sense of security and place in the world. The world becomes an unsafe and dangerous place, full of uncertainties and fears. At this time, men do crazy things and become very unpredictable in their behaviour. It is also a dangerous time. Men do crazy *things to themselves, to the woman who abandons them, and when very disturbed, even to the children they have brought into the world together. Quite frequently, men attack the woman leaving them, in a desperate attempt to put off their abandonment terror and keep hold of them. Their inner terror is of not being able to exist without the woman/lover/mother who is leaving them. A man, who appears stable and strong, can collapse and feel suicidal for a short period of time. Stories with tragic outcomes from this crisis event, the abandonment terror experience, appear regularly in the newspapers and on the television. "MAN KILLS WIFE AND TWO CHILDREN, THEN DROWNS HIMSELF OVER CLIFF." Not an uncommon headline. We see these moments depicted in television soaps, dramas, films and described in novels, all the time.*

*Although men are in some sense informed and prepared for it, when it happens they are still shocked, and overwhelmed. They switch on a man's non-rational psychology at a very deep and fundamental level. A man's most basic psychological need, to feel secure, to feel loved, to feel attached, is exploded. His abandonment terror operates simultaneously in two ways: abandonment of/by his wife; abandonment of/by his children. This includes the simultaneous breakup of his **partner relationship** and the breakup of **the family circle**. His emotional world appears to be suddenly disintegrating around him, without him having any control over the process. He is moving* *from a world of apparent security into a world of apparent chaos.*

At this time, a man's psychological self belief comes under great pressure. His confidence evaporates. He is desperately unhappy and in the **shock stage of loss**. *The intensity of his reaction to the breakup, and the time it lasts, is proportional to the intensity of his attachment to his partner and children. The more he loves them the greater the shock and fear. The longer he has loved them, the longer he endures this abandonment terror-shock. A man needs his own family and best friends, at this crucial moment of loss and change in his life. He needs his best male friend to give him emotional time and support. His own family, mother, father, brothers and sisters, can all be of great help. Somehow he has to find a way to convince himself, that he still has love and he is still lovable. He needs to believe that he will recover and have his needs to love and be loved, satisfied somewhere else.*

The shock of breakup, and the abandonment terror that follows it, lasts for several days; even as much as a week. During this time, a man is beginning to learn something crucially important, for his survival and recovery. He is beginning to gain a sense of familiarity in being alone by himself. This helps him slowly to discover that his emotional survival in the world, is not entirely dependant on a woman.

Stephen Duke

When Mummies and Daddies Breakup

When mummy and daddy say they are not going to live together any more, it comes as a profound shock to the their children. The children have to struggle to begin to make their own sense of the Mummy and daddy are cross with me
Mummy and daddy think I've been bad and naughty
Mummy and daddy are going to abandon me and leave me on my own
I won't have a mummy and daddy
Mummy doesn't love daddy so I can't love daddy
Daddy doesn't love mummy so I can't love mummy
If I love mummy, daddy won't love me
If I love daddy, mummy won't love me
It's too dangerous to love anyone
I have to choose between mummy and daddy
I love mummy <u>and</u> daddy
What can I do to help mummy start loving daddy again?
What can I do to help daddy start loving mummy again?
Daddy is a bad person because he doesn't love mummy anymore
Mummy should love daddy
Will mummy still love me even though she doesn't love daddy anymore?
What can I do to be good?
What can I do to be safe?
I don't want to leave mummy
I don't want to go to school
I hate teachers but love mummy
Why can't mummy and daddy love each other again?
Mummy and daddy used to love each other so much
I feel sad
I feel angry
I feel confused and scared

All children are profoundly emotionally affected by the break up of their parents. Their parents and the family have provided safety, continuity of care and security to them, throughout the whole of their short lives. A child attaches to each of its parents in a different way. When a parent leaves, a child's childhood is shattered. They struggle with five great emotions: **anxiety, guilt, fear, anger and loss.** *They feel anxious. They blame themselves for doing something so wrong that it might have driven a parent away. They feel angry and may become alienated from the parent who goes. At the same time they mourn the parent who has gone. Above all they mourn the loss of the circle of love. This will be true despite the unhappiness of the parents when together. Nearly all children when asked, say they want their parents to get back together again. Later, they say they wished their parents had stayed together, when they were younger.*

Divorce does not go down well with children. It is particularly difficult for children and fathers, the vast majority of whom become separated from each other for long periods of the week. **Only 1 in 20 men are given fulltime custody, or remain full-time with their children, when families breakup.** *50% of fathers then lose contact with their children altogether, within 2 years of a family breakup. Typically emotional cutoff, is a dysfunctional way for a man of surviving his shock and painful reaction to breakup and separation. Most men who cutoff and break contact with their children, are running away from the* *overwhelming pain they feel. It is a direct consequence, of the breakup of the family circle and children to whom they have become profoundly attached.*

The separation or loss of contact with father, causes deep and lasting emotional distress to sons and daughters. Shock, anxiety, anger, self-blame, mourning are all-powerful emotions that take control of a child's life for some period during this time. Children feel them, as the direct consequence of the breakup of the family and its circle of love, to which they are attached. These

"Big Five" negative emotions, will typically interfere and interrupt all the other normal processes of development, that are ongoing for a child. The age at which the divorce trauma occurs for a child therefore is highly significant. Younger children tend to lose their confidence and seek more emotional security for a time. Leaving one parent (usually mother), for contact to see father, causes them anxiety. Girls typically feel and show anxiety than boys. Boys cover up anxiety and typically show and feel more anger. They and express it either at home (towards mother), or at school towards teacher and authority. Sometimes boys express it in both places.

For teenagers, family breakup comes at a particularly difficult time. Becoming a teenager means gaining gradual independence from your parents, so that eventually you can leave home and family. If the family circle of love itself is breaking up, it makes sense that gaining independence is temporarily made more difficult. Teenagers are more aware

The Lost Patriarch

of their emotions and loyalties to each of their parents. They are more likely to feel caught in the middle between their parents. Consequently they need reassurance from both parents, that it is safe to love each of them without fear of disapproval from either.

Perhaps most damaging to children of any age, is that they can become caught up in the emotional crossfire of their separating parents. It is inevitable that in some way this will happen, even if only for a short time in the early stages. Newly separated adults will typically go through a period of emotional game playing with each other. Parents anxious about their children's loyalties to them, will subtly ask their children to take their side against the other parent. Or sometimes an angry parent will sabotage contact, between a child and the parent who has left the home. They will attempt to alienate them against the other one; usually the father. Blocking access and sabotaging contact, is especially distressing to both a father and a child, who will continue to feel emotional loyalty for their attachment to each other.

Alienation or estrangement between a father and a child is a complex area of post separation family psychology. Fortunately it occurs in only a small number of cases; 7-8%. A child, boy or girl, may refuse to see their father. He or she may close down or even cut off their emotional loyalty, as a form of self-protection against their distress of separation. They may also do this out of a fear that love may be withdrawn, by the parent with whom they still live, (usually mother), for persisting in showing "love" towards the other parent, (usually father). This dread may be amplified by the mother who for her own reasons, may consciously and deliberately emotionally alienate the child against the father. This nightmare scenario, can lead to a lasting family split. A family split has emotional consequences much further ahead in the child's lifetime.

Some children, typically boys who have an angry reaction to the break-up, can find themselves "tossed" from one separated parent to another, in episodes of conflict. Rather than being able to learn gradually, that it's okay to still love mummy and daddy, and move between their two new homes safely, the opposite occurs. They find themselves sent away to the father's home, without negotiation or routine. Here in effect, the child becomes an emotional weapon, in the hands of a distraught mother who cannot manage their son's behaviour. This is a nightmare scenario compared to one they want to remember. All this is destructive to the emotional wellbeing of children, who are struggling to accept and adapt to the separation of their parents. They want to remember their childhood, when all the family was always happy together and mummy and daddy loved each other all the time.

Divorce: An Emotional Holocaust for Men

When men are forced to undergo a divorce, (or separate from long term partners with whom they have co-habited and made a family), they experience the following extremes

> **SLEEP DISTURBANCE**
> **WEIGHT LOSS**
> **SELF CRITICAL THOUGHTS**
> **EMOTIONAL PAIN**
> **LOSS OF SELF BELIEF**
> **ABANDONMENT ANXIETY**
> **LONGING FOR UNCONDITIONAL LOVE**
> **MOURNING**

A man's masculinity and identity is challenged and he undergoes a personal crisis. Below is the outline of a healing ritual that will be of use at such a time of turnaround and recovery.

A SEPARATION DIVORCE HEALING RITUAL

(Find somewhere quiet outside in the garden. Select important possessions that symbolise your time together with your partner. Arrange them in three groups in a line in front of you. Each group represents one of the three stages: **Separation: Ashes: Re-Birth.** *Make your way down the line as you speak the words out aloud.)*

STAGE 1

Separation from your partner

"This is a time of the
taking back
OF LOVE
OF APPROVAL
OF APPRECIATION
OF BELONGING
OF INTIMACY AND KINDNESS
OF CARE AND NURTURE
OF PARTNERSHIP
OF SEX
OF CO-OWNERSHIP
OF SHARING
OF JOURNEYING
AS MAN AND WOMAN
TOGETHER"

The Lost Patriarch

STAGE 2

THE TIME OF ASHES

(Choose objects that powerfully symbolise your family together as the circle of love: (photos, toys, clothes, cd's) You have to face the pain of your loss, in order to begin the process of healing.)

Move slowly and sit among these objects and reflect;
**NO MORE OF THE FAMILY CIRCLE HOLDING HANDS
OF QUIET NIGHTS SPENT TOGETHER
OF THE LAUGHTER OF CHILDREN AT HOME
FAMILY HOLIDAYS
SCHOOLDAYS
THE TIME OF EMPTY BEDROOMS
OF FEAR
OF LONLINESS
OF ABANDONMENT
OF CRAZINESS
OF DEATH**

STAGE 3

TIME OF REBIRTH

Sit
with your self and
think forward and visualize
these things

OF COMING ALIVE

OF NURTURING CHILDREN

OF NEW PERSONALITY

OF FUTURE POTENTIAL UNFOLDING

OF NEW ACHIEVEMENT

OF BEAUTIFUL LOVERS

OF SELF RELIANCE

OF ENLIGHTENMENT

STAGE 3

TIME OF REBIRTH

Separation and Mourning

When a man separates from his wife and his family, there follows a painful, unhappy and distressing period of **MOURNING**. He has to reflect on the past, on the precious things to which he has been attached and has now lost. He continues to reach out for them for a time (sometimes a long time), in a powerful and irrational hope that somehow he can get them back. Slowly he begins to learn how to live independently in a new way. The letting go and grieving process between a man and a woman, are difficult and complicated. At the center of the divorce transition is the process of un-attaching. For a man this means experiencing the withdrawal of the love, that he has always wanted to be unconditional

When a man is a baby boy, he learns to need and depend on the unconditional love from his mother. A man is born to be her little prince, and she likes to continually please him. As I described in an earlier chapter, because of this he grows up with a lasting addictive dependency on this unconditional mother love. He then transfers that need onto his wife/partner when he meets and marries her. She becomes both mother substitute and love goddess to him. Like all addicts, when the drug of unconditional mother love is taken away, he experiences a desperate withdrawal reaction. Although in a post feminist world a partner's love *is now always conditional, when it is withdrawn, his longing for un-conditional love reveals itself and that it has never truly left him!*

A marriage ending means the loss not only of the love goddess and companion. Perhaps hardest of all, is the withdrawal of the <u>supportive love</u> which a man has come to need and depend on so badly. She is the woman who admires and adores him when he behaves like a hero; or even more importantly, when he fails. When he feels like an unsuccessful non achiever, she will say:

"Don't worry, I'll still love you. To me your still my special guy!" Her loyalty has become almost a part of his ego. Now it is broken away; and he has to find his own new separate ego and identity in the world, without her. At a time of separation and divorce, a man gets overwhelmed by this desperate pain and longing, for all these reasons. **THIS IS THE NORM**. *The pain, the loss, the going away, the withdrawal and lasting absence of this conditional/unconditional mother love and his sex goddess. Added all together it is a great deal of loss! A man still goes off to become a hero, and he learns to enjoy and rely on that comfort and safety from his partner/wife when he returns home. When he loses it after having it, and goes through a divorce, he longs to get it back, or find it again as soon as possible.*

The Lowest Point

There comes a moment during the psychological process of a divorce, when a man enters **The Pit**. *There* he reaches his grimmest, darkest, loneliest and potentially most destructive depths. For a short time, he descends emotionally and morally into his own very personal "black hole." In The Pit, he is confronted by the terrifying triple monsters of:

Abandonment, Separation Rejection.

Again and again, he now finds himself in a desperate place. He struggles through each hour of each day, guided on some automatic pilot of survival. Time becomes stretched and seems pitilessly, to go on forever. Sitting in a café, he watches the warm, comfortable intimate family exchanges of others. He feels himself in an alien emotional universe. Having to witness the tender interactions of other couples, families, children, tortures him even further. Escaping temporarily, he can only return to the womblike comfort of his bed, listening to his most comforting music. He lies there in total emotional and social paralysis, isolated from the world outside. There, his mood swings between self-destruction and murderous vengeance seeking, upon the person whom he feels has caused him this pain and suffering. The living of life has become truly unbearable.

It some ways it is surprising that so few actual acts of violence (suicide or the attacks on others), are actually committed by men at this emotionally disturbed moment of their lives. It is a regular piece of news, to read about a man *trapped in this crazy making lowest point, who has killed himself. Even worse is to read in the newspapers about another who sought vengeance through physical violence on his ex-wife in some way. The worst stories are of the very few men who set fire to their former home, sometimes with his former wife and children asleep inside it. This is the darkest tragedy that can happen. These men are in a temporary psychosis, triggered by their experience of abandonment, separation and rejection. When a man in that state, discovers the murderous consequences of his crazed actions, he usually completes the domestic/divorce tragedy by taking his own life.*

Fortunately for everyone's wellbeing, most of men learn to survive this most dangerous of times. At this dark emotional crisis point in his life, a man has to seek out and receive the emotional help and nurturing support of his closest family and friends. Their nurturing support is a crucial factor for his survival. He has to quickly learn how to use their contact and nurturing comfort, to provide a framework for his wellbeing. This also means finding a way to release his inner pain.

Men use a combination of psychological mechanisms to survive at this time. Because of the toughness/weakness syndrome from which men still suffer from patriarchy, men struggle to feel and express their pain and grief authentically. It is easier for a man to get angry than actually to feel, endure and overcome his deep emotional pain of separation and loss.

The Angry Cut Off: *fifty percent of men lose contact with their children within two years of a family break-up and divorce. This kind of man expresses his anger by emotionally punishing in return, those who he sees have abandoned <u>him</u>. That includes his innocent children. This is a highly destructive form of emotional revenge taking. It has long lasting psychological consequences for his children. Depending on their age, they have to find their own solutions to <u>his</u> unjustifiable abandonment of <u>them.</u> This effect of his cut off, endures through the lifetime of his children, inevitably scarring their own attachment experience, self worth and sense of being loveable.*

Counter Ecstasy Seeking: *Using the powerful psychological defence mechanism of Denial, many men compulsively attempt to start celebrating life again. Substance abuse, alcohol dependency, sexual promiscuity and overwork, are all great temporary comfort providers. They can distract from the process of healing to some extent. Centred however around the core process of denying their reality, these behaviours mask the inner emotional truth of a man's, anger, sadness, fear and pain. Eventually he has to abandon these artificial comforters, if he is to begin the authentic process of self-healing. All of these things are compulsive behaviours to avoid beginning the emotional work, so vital to his recovery and further growth as a man.*

Self Healing

The emotional psychological work, following the pain of a divorce and family break-up, concerns "going inwards." Slowly, bit by bit allowing himself to begin to **feel again**, *this becomes possible for a man. When he allows himself to enter this dark cave, he slowly emerges from the divorce experience genuinely healed and iron willed, in his determination to survive. He allows himself to both experience his anger about what has happened, but also to feel the true intensity of his fears and painful grief.* **Here are some self more healing techniques:**

> *[1]Talking intimately to close friends:* (divorcing men have to learn to talk to each other, about their emotional distress. This challenges the "be tough myth of manhood".
> *[2] Walk-Exercise* **(Healing the Body helps heals he Mind)**
> *[3]Write/Draw/Paint* **(Find a way to use words and images to describe your state of mind and heart)**
> *[4] Music* **(Listening/playing/composing music are great healers.)**
> *[5] Meditate* **(Take up a new form of meditation such as yoga or tai chi.)**
> *[6] Gardening. Building. Making.*

Writing his own healing poetry, talking to close friends, listening and playing music, walking, painting, meditation; all of these are the " cathartic " healing arts that enable this healthy process of emotional learning and recovery.

Despite the difficulties described above, there is an immense emotional opportunity for men who are experiencing a divorce. A man can emerge from what is an overwhelming male life crisis, emotionally stronger and knowing himself better. Gradually, however difficult because of it, more understanding of his own love psychology can emerge. Heroism and achievement comes easy to men. Learning about love is much harder for them, hence the chaos and breakdown we currently see in the male female relationship.

Manhood and Emotional Self Reliance

Developing his emotional intelligence, (his capacity to express and manage his feelings), is a crucial chapter in a man's epic life story. It is an essential part of a man's journey through Life. It is the beginning of the slow transformation from the self seeking hero, into a compassionate being of love. There is a crucial aspect of this emotional learning that begins through divorce. It is a time when he can finally learn to let go of his dependant longing for unconditional woman-mother love. By doing this he can start to achieve real emotional self-reliance. To become more truly emotionally **Self** *reliant, a man has firstly have to work on* **healing his hurt**. *He has to find a way to merge the Iron and his Soul. To begin this process of finding a deep inner stable manhood, a man has to learn to tune into the INTERNAL MOTHER who lives* **inside** *men, as well as the IRON MAN we all know so well. The Internal Mother is put there by the hundreds of thousands of hours of emotional memory that a man has of his* **real mother**. *Her quiet soothing voice, can provide him with all the comfort, softness, security and unconditional love that he could wish for. A man has to be prepared to learn to tune into her. She has a quiet soft voice. It is can often be the voice of his own real mother. Listening to her, he can begin to receive all the things that a mother's unconditional love can give him:*

Exercise:
1. **Go to a quiet place. Breathe slowly. Tune deep inside yourself.**
2. **Start to listen to a quiet female voice that will come to you.**
3. **Listen to and receive the nurturing energies of that voice**

Allow yourself to tune into and receive these aspects of your feminine self.

> SELF
> ACCEPTANCE
> COMFORT
> EMOTIONAL WARMTH
> NURTURING KINDNESS
> ENCOURAGEMENT
> RECOGNITION
> CALMNESS
> SECURITY

Learning to recognise, receive and constantly tune into this feminine part of his own masculine nature, is a crucial aspect of what we now call the New Masculinity. Most men are good at learning about the Iron; the tough, the hard, the durable. We grow this inside us by learning to compete, finding achievement and trying to become a hero in our own ways. Being alone with ourselves provides this opportunity to grow this other aspect of our psychological nature; to discover a more complete and holistic balance of our masculinity.

When a break-up or divorce happens, a man will often panic and think: "I have to find another woman with whom I can share my life" What this is really about is his compulsive need to express his dependant longing on the female. This can often be a great mistake, as the statistics of second marriages show.(Five out of ten fail!). Instead, he can say calmly to himself: "No. I will take time to find my own emotional way in the world." This is a commitment to discovering the emotional self reliance needed in the new world of post patriarchy. Growing up emotionally, being able to look after himself, (with the help of his male friends and family), marks a new step forward in his life.

Post Patriarchy and Parent-Child Bonding

In the new post patriarchal family, there are enormous changes emerging in the patterns of parenting and childcare. Most men I meet, say they spend more time with their own children than their fathers did with them. Many say they want and intend to spend even more time with their children, than they already do. Mothers who work, (i.e. four out of five with dependant age children), can therefore reasonably expect fathers to take increasing responsibility for their children. Many men seem to be up for the opportunity and challenge. This means that more and more children are and will attach, with equal intensity and depth to both their fathers and mothers. This **new co-equal**

The Lost Patriarch

attachment psychology, *is at the emotional heart of the post patriarchal family. This will increasingly have enormous emotional repercussions, when* **fathers and mothers can no longer live with each other, and families break up**. *The new co-equality of parent-child attachment grows during and continues after a family breakup occurs. Children and fathers, who have strongly bonded through spending lots of nurture/play time together, do not suddenly become non attached or un-attached. When couples separate and decide to break up,* **the family circle of love, has to be reorganized.** *Following the breakup of the new post patriarchal family circle, the immediate priority is to create two homes. Contact needs to be quickly established in which children can spend an fair proportion of time with each parent.*

The co-equal couple is a new and revolutionary concept and also an emerging reality in gender psychology. The co-equal couple are at the centre of this emerging family model. They freely swap and interchange their roles as providers and nurturers. A women works and rests, while a man provides childcare and nurtures the children; and vice versa. When divorce and family break-up happens, the law needs to recognise and adapt to the new changing reality in family attachment psychology. Father-child and child-father bonding now has a new depth, intensity and loyalty that cannot be interrupted in the old patriarchal ways following divorce. The patriarchal father was then tossed outside the newly reshaped family circle, and forced to become an emotionally peripheral figure. Children visited at best on alternate week-ends and some holidays. This is no longer a balanced and stabilizing reaction to the trauma of family breakup.

In the post patriarchal 21st century family, the equality of a father's love for his children is expressed in new and fundamental ways. His increased levels of child contact time and the joys of nurturing his children, now match those of most mothers. As a consequence bonding and attachment loyalties between father and children, will increasingly have a new intensity and depth. So now when families break up, a child's emotional loyalties will belong equally to both parent. A very unhappy father once said to me, "The system does not understand men like me: nurturers and homemakers. It treats us shamefully when our families breakup." The custody/contact law has reflected the past patriarchal psychology of families, when a mother was the **primary attachment figure.** Fathers of co equal partnerships which then break-up, possess the emotional and nurturing skills to create their own household and circle of love as single parents.

Fathers, who become involved nurturers with their kids, want and need to stay involved with their kids. When couples break up, families have to reorganise and find how to be together in a new way. The law needs to reflect this emotional change, and give equal custody to fathers and mothers who have been equal carers.

Should they both work more or less?
Does the woman want to work more or less?
Do the woman or man want children or not?
What is the right amount of time to be together as a couple?
How much time do the woman or man want to be on their own, or with their friends?
How much time does the woman and the man
want with the children?

More and more, men who are deeply attached to their children will fight for contact and equal custody, following family breakup. Post patriarchy is more about nurturing patterns of male parenting (in contrast to a provider pattern of male parenting). It seeks to continue deeply involved contact between fathers and children, despite a breakup between parents. There are more changes ahead, as the fundamental shift in male attachment psychology from provider to nurturer/provider continues.

Healing the Circle of Love

I have spoken with many men about their feelings as fathers, as their families are breaking up or when they have broken up. Most of them are unable or unwilling to describe the full intensity of their feelings to me. After families do break-up, more and more fathers are struggling to maintain more contact; two, three or more days a week with their children. This reflects the domestic and emotional truth, that fathers are now more and more co-equal carers within the home. This is the case from when children are born, and then on continuously during family life. As a result of this much more active role of fathers, in providing nurture (emotional security), as well as income (material security), intensely strong and loyal attachments are formed between fathers and their children. Family break-up comes as a truly shattering blow to all concerned. The pain of this break-up for men (and children) is initially unbearable. The longing for contact goes unfulfilled, daily, hour by hour. The absence of a child, no longer there to hold, speak to, play with, cook for, eat with, do homework with, kiss good night, take to football, watch television with, read to, take to the shops, go swimming with, answer questions to; leaves a vast, black hole of emotional longing. The priority for a father *overwhelmed by his unbearable separation, is to work hard at* **creating his own new family circle.** *The old family circle has gone; the imperative is to make a new circle with himself and children.*

Men still believe in marriage: Women less so?

There is a crisis in marriage the likes of which has never been seen before. Even so, men still keep committing themselves to a woman through marriage. Four out of five men have been married by the age of 30. Although almost half of those marriages are over within 5 years, the majority of men then go on and remarry a different woman within 2 years! So it is not a case of once bitten twice shy. Men are still very keen to try and live in a marriage. When a man has found a woman who combines enough of the love goddess and earth mother, he wants to try and keep her. He wants to "tie the knot" around her and himself. Something very primal in manhood still seeks security, belonging, loyalty, homemaking. Love, marriage, tying the knot, all still seem to go together. So marriage still seems to be what the majority of men want. Marriage, commitment, fatherhood, all affirm a man powerfully in his traditional, primal masculinity. His "old fashioned manhood" can still be deepened and strengthened by the promise of a life commitment. But when he is confronted within the marriage by the changes that post feminism demands, men fall away in their millions!

From a love point of view, the best things happen in twos. We are a species that bonds in couples and twos. When we truly bond, we still seem to want to bond for life with one person. The patriarchal fairy tale seems to be hanging on with great stubbornness and determination. The search for the perfect partner and marriage, remains deeply active in men. Psychologically men enter marriage full of expectation, positively motivated for a lasting outcome. What goes wrong? Why does marriage become a battlefield on which so many couples are blown apart? Most importantly, in the emerging psychology of manhood, what might men be able to change about themselves to stop that?

The first thing that often makes a marriage go wrong, is that a man goes into it before he has enough heroic achievement in his own life. For a man, his urgent selfish search for heroic achievement, usually limits his capacity to love a woman. He needs first to do enough of the hero stuff for himself. Study, career, playing football, writing music, or walking to all the corners of the world. All the numerous but hero making actions that affirm his manhood. Doing these in sufficient quantities, gives him a better chance of learning how to love within the co-equal relationship. So the rule has to be: wait until you feel enough of a hero, before you marry! Generally speaking, a "too early" man marries before feeling sufficiently confirmed in his own manhood by his achievement. This achievement immaturity can mean it is harder for him to accept the rules, of the new post patriarchal marriage from the beginning. The post-feminist partner is more and more concerned with the fulfilment of her own achievement psychology. This will

The Lost Patriarch

include before and after motherhood, her need to achieve her own potential in career and other terms.

In the new world of post patriarchy, more and more couples do not need to go through with a "marriage." 40% of children are now born to unmarried parents in the United Kingdom; a percentage that is increasing year on year. This is a cultural revolution in the old morality of living together in sin. It is a social and family pattern, in total contrast to that of forty years ago, before the final explosion of feminism. Men and women who are committed enough to live with each other and start a family, see marriage as belonging to some other generation. For more and more couples, marriage seems to a ritual that belongs very much to the former world of patriarchy, which men created. Post patriarchy is much more the outcome of the liberating force of women. Many couples now mistrust the ties and obligations that accompany marriage. They even look upon marriage as an obstacle to their intimacy and happiness as a committed relationship.

More about Lessons in Love for Men

Although many families now break up (4 in 10 in the first five years), many re-form in different combinations. Four out of five men, find another partner within 2 years of a divorce or breakup. Sadly, the failure rate of second or third re-marriages is even higher; 5 out of 10 or 50% of them go on and fail. It seems that although men often decide they do not wish to stay with one particular woman, that does stop their search for another women. Separated men

Stephen Duke

seem to rush out and become deeply involved with another one very quickly. Have they given themselves time to find answers to the questions: what have I learned from before? Has anything changed inside me? Will I go off and repeat the same patterns and behaviors with another woman, and will the whole emotional endeavor fail again?

It is not uncommon now, to find a man who has been divorced two, three times or more. The relationship between men and women continues to be a very unstable one. A couple will only stay together, when the balance of their needs is maintained enough of the time. Knowing enough about how to maintain this balance, has become more and more difficult for men to understand. Men are confused about what they should be doing more of, or less of, to keep the balance safe, enough of the time. What is the combination of behaviors that will work for the co-equal couple?

**Should they both work more or less?
Does the woman want to work more or less?
Do the woman or man want children or not?
What is the right amount of time to be together as a couple?
How much time do the woman or man want to be on their own, or with their friends?
How much time does the woman and the man
want with the children?**

When a marriage or a long-term partnership ends, it is time for a serious life review. A man needs to take time and reflect carefully. He should allow himself time to think long and hard, about what was his own contribution to the relationship breakup. This requires a lot of emotional honesty. He has to find a way through these negative experiences, and learn to face with unflinching honesty, the reality of his own behaviour.

Anger is a particularly obstructive emotion to overcome, and it blocks this creative process of reflection.

1. *Anger: blocks out the pain of loss and the withdrawal of love. Instead this needs to be felt, mourned and faced up to.*
2. *Anger: hides the identity confusion and uncertainty of life purpose, that inevitably occurs for a man, when his long term partnership breaks up.*
3. *Anger: enables most or all of the emotional responsibility for the breakup, to be placed on the other person, THE EX.*
4. *Anger can hinder, delay and perhaps postpone for the rest of his life, a man's opportunity for learning the lessons of love.*

Heroism, or the search for it, still comes relatively easy for men. Finding and maintaining a long term relationship, learning intimacy and attachment are still the most difficult things for them to learn about. When long term relationships break down and come to an end, the great opportunity for learning about intimacy and attachment are there to be taken.

Men are rightly becoming more and more concerned, with the responsibility they have for their self development. This is a crucially important and empowering process for a man; **and it takes time.** *After a marriage or partnership breakdown, much of this process of learning, self discovery, growth and change is best done alone and in the company of other close male friends. Only men can provide each other with the "healing workshop", they each need to make this progress. If instead, a man seeks to re-attach himself unchanged to another woman, then he will face the same issues about relationship, intimacy and attachment with her. He will then get trapped in a succession of relationships, that play out the same unresolved patterns. Over driven hero/ achiever; the self-centered male; the constant expectation for and taking of love; angry responses to a woman's co-equal expectations; the inability to give to and nurture others. These are the typical problems men struggle with in the journey of love. This is the psychological agenda in the passage from self-seeking hero into compassionate man of love. The lessons of loving for a man that enable future change for him in other loving attachments are:*

> 1. *Talk. Be open. Let a dialogue about who does what flow between you.*
> 2. *Learn to live more from the heart as well as the head.*
> 3. *Show attention and give attentiveness,*
> 4. *Be empathic. Let your feelings guide you about what others feel.*
> 5. *Search for a co-equal balance.*
> 6. *Seek your own particular work-life balance together.*
> 7. *Explore what it means to live in a home of domestic democracy.*
> 8. *Find softness in strength and strength in softness.*
> 9. *Understand your machismo for what it is; tough, primal, primitive, and something brought from your evolutionary past.*
> 10. *Recognise her need to be an achiever/hero as much as your own.*

The Divorced Man in Singledom

For a man, becoming single again after a lengthy period of marriage, is like suddenly finding yourself in a foreign country with no passport, unable to speak the local lingo and no map reading skills! Very quickly you have to work out where you are, what everyone else is doing, what language they speak and the many dangers to avoid.

Rule 1.
Learn to accept and feel comfortable being alone.

The first thing is learning to be alone. Afters years of marriage, and being accustomed to a constant female companion and the noisy comforting presence of children, you suddenly discover BEING ALONE. You sleep alone, get up alone, come home to an empty house, you eat alone and you watch a movie on television, alone. You now find yourself becoming overdosed, on the very thing you craved for most when married; more time by yourself! If you are not careful, you can find yourself drowning in a vast ocean of aloneness. At this point a lot of men will rush out in anguish, searching to find an instant replacement for their ex-partner or wife. Afraid and freaked out by the emptiness in their new single life, they try to replace it too quickly with another relationship. This kind of emotional panic has two neurotic motives: firstly to block out and deny the immense loss and pain at relationship and family break-up: secondly to try and avoid the new reality of being alone.

Divorce is a death;
let yourself die in order to come alive again.

Now is the moment in your new single life, to face the fear and panic all men feel at this moment in their lives. It is the fear and panic that a man will feel, when confronted for the first time **with becoming fully responsible for**

himself. *As a man, you will have relied very much on a woman up to this point in your life, to support and nurture you emotionally and domestically. From that first desperate angry breath, taken after the escape from the womb of your mother; to falling into the arms of your first love goddess; to creating a family with your partner or wife, you will have learned to enjoy the dependant comfort of her nurture. Now it is time to grow up emotionally and learn to nurture yourself. At last, in your thirties, forties or fifties, you can embrace the opportunity of learning to become emotionally and domestically self sufficient. I am not saying, give up women or become sexually abstinent: (more on that later). What I am saying, is:*

begin to wean yourself from the dependency on women that you have been conditioned into believing you must have,

from the moment you were born!

Rule 2.
Learn how to become a Domestic God

If you did not make this transition in your marriage, and you relied on your ex-female partner to do the washing, buy the groceries, clean the kitchen, replace the toilet paper, wash the loos, iron the laundry, vacuum the carpets, cook the meals, choose the colours for the curtains and bedding, wash the fridge, select the cleaning materials at the super market and defrost the freezer: now is your once in a lifetime opportunity, to become a Domestic God. Embrace it now and celebrate your manhood in a new way. You will grow and become more complete as a man.

The end of female domination of the domestic universe is at hand!

If you did become a domestic god during the marriage, now you can learn to become a more complete one. Most men are natural homemakers. Learn the many pleasures and deep sense of satisfaction that can be gained, from spending a weekend homemaking. Cooking, cleaning, tidying, gardening, washing and tendering to your own home.

Rule 3.
Discover Male Emotional and Sexual Liberation

There is very little discussed or written about the idea that men can and need to become more sexually liberated. It is assumed (probably by men themselves and women as well), that they are and have always been sexually liberated. In a patriarchy, they either get their sexual needs met at home, or went out looking for gratification elsewhere: or did both! Is being compulsively driven throughout your life by the Rampant Sex God, true male sexual liberation? Or is being equally intoxicated in the opposite way by the Love Prince, during the falling-in-love experience, true male sexual liberation? Both are states of mind and body over which, a man has little or no control. In both states he is being driven and compelled from within, with little or no sense of freedom, choice and self determination.

Learning to live alone in the new land of singledom and aloneness is sexually a very creative time. We have explored how sex in marriage nearly always becomes involved in bargaining and trade offs between a couple. Many women (and research over the last two decades definitely confirms this) gradually lose interest in sex with their long term male partner. They continue to masturbate and fantasise regularly about their sexual fantasy figures: film actors, footballers, pop singers, colleagues, male friends. But sex with their male partner becomes less and less important on their day-to-day agenda. Unfortunately or fortunately depending on your view, it remains very high on the male agenda.

This is not the case for the newly divorced man in singledom. Initially alone, he has to rely primarily on masturbation to express and satisfy his sex drive. Learning to masturbate as often as he wants, and thinking about whomever he chooses to think about, is an important stage in his new sexual liberation. Our sexual manhood begins in adolescence when we encounter our first true love goddess. She switches on the twin sex gods within us: the Rampant Inner sex God and the Love Prince. Our first sexual liberation is an instinctive, unconscious process over which we have little or no control. We are spellbound and captured by her erotic power. Now in our new older, wiser, post marital single state, we can begin to become more familiar with our twin sex gods and their highly contrasting *power and energies. The fantasies we play out in our rituals of masturbation, can help us in this liberating process. Get to know the twin sex gods and the very different moods and energies they arouse in you. Learn to master them, rather than the other way round. When a man can begin to do this, he can have more understanding and choice about the kinds of women who turn him on sexually. Reflecting carefully on the kind of woman to whom he is now being attracted, will continue this process of sexual self-awareness and self-knowledge.*

Divorce is a death and rebirth. This is very much the case with a man's sexuality. In a marriage, a man learns to channel his sexuality through one woman. Over the years of creating a common sexual language together, he and his partner create a sex life, unique to them. When they separate, that sex life dies as well. This is often traumatic to a man's sexuality in the early stage of break up. He may temporarily lose his sexual confidence, doubts his sexual powers, and become uncertain of his sexual attractiveness to other women. He has to learn to begin again, from the basics. Initially, it is like going back to the early years of adolescence, when he was a sexual beginner. After the emotional disaster of break-up, most men initially seek out a **female sexual healer.** *This woman plays a very important role in emotionally healing his wounded heart; and crucially, she reassures him about his sexual prowess. Her kind open heart and body, enable his sex gods to be reborn after the disaster of a lost love life of marriage.*

Rule 4.
Learn to explore the Sexual Field

There are now a great many free, liberated and unattached women. If a man can grow up emotionally, and learn to live the life of singledom, he can take his time to explore his sexuality with women. By doing this he can get to know and understand his twin sex gods with more insight.

If a man follows these rules, (for a minimum of two years after break-up), then he will have time to learn about himself in the new world of singledom. Divorce is death and a disaster when you are going through it. When you have negotiated its tortuous passages, it can and will provide deep emotional and sexual insights into who you are, and who you are becoming as a man. It is crucial that a man takes this time, to reflect. It will pave the way to a new self knowledge and independence, that can be truly liberating for him.

Male Types: Piers Public School

P is for Piers. P is also for privilege. I have met Piers in many different contexts of life. Although overstuffed with privilege, he is a both a shallow and a noble fellow. His existence is sustained by the belief that his class still rules the world; in spirit and values if not in substance. His hero psychology is comfortably expressed, in the "natural" leadership of his class and race. The fragile tower of his male ego and his self confidence, flourish within that now self deceiving myth. He flows with ease into the conventional professions of law, medicine, city business, the army. Achievement is easy for him within these conventional professions. He accepts with ease the obligations of his family and social background.

The public school system is a system of conformity and convention, where first and foremost, men learn how to do what they are told by other men. When you meet Piers Public School, he will probably be charming to you. However, this charm is quite superficial. It is a handsome social mask, perfected over many years of learning and practice, from early boyhood. Above all, it will disguise who he really is and prevent any opportunity for closeness, and heaven forbid INTIMACY. In his own exclusive and private circle of other male friends, friendships between men are maintained by sharing the old fashioned values of male chauvinism and the more trendy aspects of bloke-ishness. This includes communal drinking, watching and playing sport, competing at work, the sharing of sexual anecdotes about women, and mostly the subtle bragging about property ownership and income. Within Piers there also lingers a dark and shadowy racism that condescends and looks down upon every other caste, class, race and culture in the world. Piers is an historical throwback. He belongs to a former age of empire, a belief in the myth of racial supremacy of the white race, and above all the patriarchal dominance of men over women. If you are born into this class the male journey of becoming is more difficult.

CHAPTER 6:
War and Games

"Rugby to me is the ultimate team sport. Its physical nature and requirements of courage and bravery, as well as skill, develop a camaraderie that sets it apart. I often compare how we feel together in those moments before kick off, to how a soldier might feel before a battle."
                    Johnny Wilkinson: England rugby hero.

Parallel Occupations of the Male

<u>To the male of the species; sport is war and war can be sport.</u>
<u>War and Games have some COMPELLING parallels.</u>
Here they are:

Both involve the 'Team' or 'Company'
Both invite extremes of physical bravery
In both you can ' neutralize the opposition '
Both offer opportunities for heroism and decoration:
e.g.Military Cross vs Man of the Match
Both combine individual skills with a team purpose
Both seek "Victory"
Both enable intense attachment/bonding between males,
Both suppress the soft feminine side in a man
Both release the killer warrior instincts inside a man

Stephen Duke

SPORT AND WAR

Deep inside every man are warrior instincts, that come from our very ancient history as human hunters. The experience of thousands of generations, of using male courage against animals and out in the wilderness of Nature, is encoded within our male genes. These are instincts that are still active in manhood behaviour. This psycho-evolutionary programming, to search out danger and challenges, against which we can pit our bravery, is powerfully imprinted into us. In this way we discover and tune into the darker side of our manhood, and some part of the killer breed we have always been. Although in civilized times, warfare is not for the majority and we oppose its brutality and inhumanity, most men still do sport.

Playing Games Together and Male Bonding

It is naïve to believe that 100,000 generations of primal male evolution, can be washed away from our genes by political correctness and the emerging patterns of post patriarchy. To have any chance of changing **who** we are, we have to recognise **what** we are.

There is no doubt that sport is the most civilised alternative to war, created by men. It re-directs the powerfully aggressive instincts that still flow through all men. The truth is that underneath, all men still belong to a warlike species. To begin to understand ourselves now as men, we have to face the truth of this. Only then can we begin to see ourselves and our current manhood. There is a tradition of violence, killing, warfare and hatred that still remains powerfully alive today in all human cultures. We have first to recognise as individual men, that we have been born into this evolutionary context, in order to be able to begin to distinguish our own separate identity from it.

The habit of warfare, has developed particularly over the last three hundred years. It was during that period of our history, that it really got going. Behind it lay an overpowering belief in the myth of: "The White Master Race". This myth justified the invasion, murder and enslavement of any other race whose country and wealth the white race wanted to possess. Behind these centuries of barbarism, lay the delusion that the rest of the world were "savages". That our race, culture and "civilization" were superior to everyone else, and our God was the only true God. In this way, any *guilt or shame we might have been capable of feeling, for our inhumanity to countless millions of other men women and children, was overcome by believing that we were actually bringing "enlightenment to the world." This compulsion for conquest, was and remains the darkest aspect of masculinity and patriarchy. The psychological priority for post patriarchy, is to find a new global myth that embraces with joy, the power and equality of all races and cultures. We need a view of the world that respects the cultures and inheritance of all indigenous peoples, whom we can accept as* **different and equal.**

Most men who do not actually have to take part in the wars that regularly come along, (now the vast majority us), work off our appetite for potential violence by taking part in the great civilised alternative to war: Games.

Heroism, Manhood and War

In the film series "Band of Brothers" produced by Stephen Spielberg and Tom Hanks, there is a scene which tells us a lot about this aspect of our male psychology. A sergeant is speaking to a private soldier, who he discovers shaking and paralyzed with fear, in a ditch by the front line. In a previous scene in the film, we have already seen the soldier experiencing a temporary hysterical blindness during a previous contact with the enemy, whom he was unable to see. His terrified mind had told him he could not see the enemy, and his eyes believed it. The sergeant looking at the soldier says:

The Lost Patriarch

"Until you recognise there is no hope, and that you are already dead, you will not be able to act without mercy, compassion or remorse and do what you have to do. Fight you bastard."

This scene helps us get an insight into two very different types of men, whose manhood is exposed to the extreme conditions of battle in war. The sergeant is the kind of man who can do his warrior stuff in the setting of war so well, that he can be decorated as a hero. Somehow he has been able to accept his "emotional death" and that there is no hope for his life. Being able to do that, he can transform himself into an emotionally cut-off killer. This enables him to survive psychologically on the battlefield. It means he has become a merciless killer in battle. He does not experience fear when faced with death. He feels no compassion for the other men, the enemy, and feels no guilt about what he does to them.

In complete contrast, the psychology of the other man, the private soldier under his command is disturbed. He has not been able to switch off his emotional attachment to life, and the contact he has made with his compassionate, feminine side. His feeling feminine side is in conflict with the brutal war and its random killing. Psychologically he is fighting against the war; not in it. He is both angry at it and terrified by it. He wants to smell the flowers, look at the sky, be at home with his family and wife. As a consequence he experiences the kind of psychological phenomena not uncommon with men in battle: a paralysing fear and hysterical

Stephen Duke

blindness. He is overwhelmed by his compassionate concern for the other men blown apart by bullets and shells. He is tuned in by his empathy to their terror, pain and struggle for survival.

Eventually his disturbed psychological condition, results in him breaking down. He wants to be part of the Band of Brothers, but killing is too difficult for him. He cannot take the step into becoming a warrior. When the new battle does begin, he starts to fire his rifle. He joins the rest of the soldiers in battle. But he is weeping uncontrollably in distress, as he shoots wildly into thin air. Finally he actually shoots another man, the enemy, and tries to proclaim himself a warrior. But as a result he becomes even crazier, driven psychotic by his sense of guilt and shame at what he has done.

Some interesting psychological research came out of the Second World War. It suggested that the vast majority of men in battle, were deliberately **shooting to miss, not to hit and kill the enemy soldiers.** This implied that most men, consciously or unconsciously, despite their warrior training, did not want to kill other men. Appalled by this, the US Army, hired the behavioral psychologist BF Skinner. Skinner was an expert in conditioning techniques, that train an automatic behavioral response in people. His instructions were clear: train the reflexes of our human soldiers so that they became killing machines. The army did not want their soldiers exercising their emotional or moral judgment as men, in any way on the battlefield. The army wanted to be a vast killing organization. Each individual soldier, was thus conditioned to be a tiny part of that killing whole.

The Killing Breed

What is clear from this story and the real world, is that men who experience war and killing, are changed forever. A small number of " happy killers" enter the world of the warrior. They can go on killing and they can function for a considerable time as effective soldiers in the world of slaughter and mayhem. They can operate as special forces, and continue to do their stuff behind enemy lines. They are a special breed, who become war heroes and military warriors. Society decorates them and we recognise that they protect us from other men like them, on the other side, the enemy. They live in a world of supreme machismo, to most of us terrifyingly detached from their feelings as they practice their profession. However even they sometimes want to pick the flowers, or read poetry and listen to music. And even they have a psychological breaking point. The character played by Brando in Apocalyse Now, is an in depth study of this kind of super warrior. He nevertheless eventually cracks and becomes a random uncontrolled psychotic killer. The army have to hire another member of special forces to go out and hunt him down to assassinate him

Throughout history, and in many cultures, the only way to manhood was as a soldier. In ancient Greece, it was the finest male honour to become the "Hoplite" who carried and used their short sword in battle. Fathers passed on their short sword to their sons. Generations of men achieved their manhood through war. Practicing the arts of warfare was honorable and highly respected. The Viking soldiers of the middle ages believed that they entered Valhalla when they died fighting in battle. Their manhood psychology believed this was the greatest honour, the greatest glory for a male warrior. They were heroes in the flesh, and then became heroes after life in the spirit world. The male terrorists, who hijacked and flew planes into the World Trade Centre, were motivated by a similar holy manhood psychology. They believed they were fighting a Gihad or Holy War. They believed that at the moment of their death, they were reborn again spiritually and could enter paradise for the "goodness of their killing deeds." In believing this, they had become the warriors who could act without mercy, compassion or remorse for their actions. Manhood and war can become a sublimely dark double act.

Exercise: 1
1. Where does the Secret Killer hang out in you?
2. How does it show itself?
3. What happens to you and what do you do?
4. How do you control it when it has "jumped out"?
5. Who does it affect most?

Exercise 2:
1. Tune out of the Secret Killer into your Heart
2. Embrace the wide polarity between the two; the Killer and the Heart

The Lost Patriarch

3. *Allow yourself to sit between the two forces, experience the two*

Dark Heart of the Killer

We men inherit from our evolutionary past, a dark primal archetype. In his book "Lord of the Flies ", the great writer William Golding explores this theme. A group of English school boys, (from both public and state schools), are stranded without teachers or adults on a desert island. Slowly but inevitably, the shallow mask of civilization drops off their faces. What emerges is a savage rivalry, superstition, fear, killing and a pagan worship of nature. This hidden killer in men, is also explored in another great novel by the writer Joseph Conrad who called his book "The Heart of Darkness".

*Many men on returning from war, are unable to settle again into civilian life. A woman I was treating in therapy, told me about some letters she had found. They had been in her attic for many years, and had been written by her dead father to her mother. They were kind, loving, supremely tender; epistles of the Love Prince to his Love Goddess, her mother. She was shocked by them, and emotionally overwhelmed. She could not understand how they could have been written by **her** father. She had known him as a disturbed, brutal alcoholic. He was unloving to her as she grew up as his young daughter. She had witnessed her father frequently hitting her mother when returning home drunk, and then smashing up the house. She had grown up terrified of him, feeling only hatred and fear. He had walked* out one day never to return to the home. She was still only a young child when it had happened and she remembered her joy and relief the day he left. When she began to read his tender letters, she felt that she had once had a good father who was a kind loving good man. A man who had once been capable of romantic love, supremely tender, kindly and emotional stable. Clearly something profound had happened to the writer of those letters to her mother. They had been written during the war, when he was away in military service in the Far East. The man who eventually returned home after the war, had by then become a very different person.

In war, men witness events that can only be described as hellish. They experience unimaginable brutality and witness their close friends die in screaming agony. They can come to believe they are in hell. Unless they are the special breed of warrior described above, they struggle to cope with the impact of the events on their mind. Returning to normal life after combat, they regularly have nightmares and cannot sleep. They have flashbacks. They become moody, depressed, anxiety ridden, paranoid. There is a whole range of physical symptoms they can experience in conjunction with these psychological ones. Now we can offer them some help and treatment for a condition we describe as Post Traumatic Stress Disorder. In the past they received no recognition of their profound disturbance. They became alcoholics to block out their feelings. Their disturbed, untreated behaviour broke up relationships and

The Lost Patriarch

families. They became brutal and bullying. They were lost. They were not made to feel as heroes of any kind. Above all many them could not return to their families, and play the roles of husband and father.

Killing Games

The field of sport and games has become a safer stage, for the warrior in a man to let out his dark energies. There he is protected by rules and codes. The young boys, (often abandoned by fathers) who come to playtherapy sessions, play out their Secret Killer in the sandtray. War games, heroes, massacres and killing stories are their favorite thing. Their play is spontaneous, impulsive and naturally there inside them. In warrior games on Playstations, which boys from the age of two or three now own, the central character is the hero/warrior/killer. His challenge is a quest, during which he often has to kills the evil enemy, that stands in the way. Once the Secret Killer becomes awake in a boy at the age of 5, 10, 15 20, it changes him. It is the complete opposite of our tender, nurturing, compassionate spiritual nature. In this very real sense, the living psychology of men is one of opposites. The masculine journey challenges us to discover a balance between them.

The contrasting human theatres of war and the sports field, are animated by similar aspects of our male psychology. Sometimes the only difference is what the men hold in their hands, and a limiting code of rules. For a cricket bat, substitute a rapier, for rugby ball, imagine a grenade or small bomb, for the javelin a machine gun that kills. In sport there are rules; in war the "rules" of contact are almost non existent, very soon they start to breakdown. There is no referee on the battlefield.

The Violence in Modern Men

For most of human history, violence has been a strictly male affair. Men fighting men; men testing their strength and bravery against one another; men killing each other. In the early days of our human history, the evolutionists tell us men killed animals and other humanoids to survive. Neanderthal Man was the ancient species most savaged by Homo Sapiens, and (we are told) eventually successfully exterminated him from the planet. Tribalism and the potential for dangerous violence that goes with it, is deep rooted in our psycho-evolutionary origins. The potential to fight, violate and even to kill, seems to be encoded in men from their evolutionary past. Despite all of the moral, civilised progress of the last few centuries, it remains at some level a fundamental aspect of masculine psychology.

Men living in a modern western culture have changed. Most do not act out violence. Very few kill. The last twentieth century highlighted the psychological change that seems to transform male behaviour during wartime. Men develop powerful psychological disturbance, and are deeply traumatised by their experiences of violence, battle and killing. They need intensive psychotherapeutic treatment for their Post Traumatic Stress Disorder. Why? What has happened to the warriors of old? Those men who gloried in violence, warfare and murderous lust for a killing victory?

The truth is modern man does not have the stomach for killing. His civilised sensibilities have outgrown his wild, hunting origins that allowed him to kill when necessary.

For a few people however, when the belief systems they hold are organised in a certain way, killing is still possible. With the powerful technologies of modern warfare and terrorism, they are even more dangerous to the rest of us that before. They are joined by a new phenomenon: warrior women.

Ultimate Warriors, Ultimate Worship

The most lethal combination known to Man on the killing fields, is the combination of a radical faith and the active psychology of the warrior hero. Terrorists can turn themselves into human bombs, sacrificing their lives in the holy cause. The 14 men who kidnapped the planes which they flew into the twin towers in New York on September 11th, did so in the contented belief that they entered Paradise at the moment of their deaths. They truly believed that their sacrificial deaths were being offered up in an act of ultimate worship and holy martyrdom. Holy war and the holy warrior has a long history. The Christian Crusades were fought in the name of a "better" God. The Kami Kazee pilots of the second world war, were "holy warriors", in the sacrificial service of their emperor God.

There is a certain kind of man (not as rare as we would wish to think), who seems able to harness his religious psychology, to his warrior instincts. Belief in a God and killing in his holy name, still remains high on the agenda in a certain male world. The killing field, (whatever its form, battlefield or terrorist act), continues to provide a public theatre for warrior glory, both heroic and spiritual. It provides the opportunity for the hero/warrior to seek out danger, confront his challenge, test his bravery and achieve heroic recognition in this life or an afterlife. As long as young men who believe in a God, also receive deep psychological motivation from the hero/warrior, then they can be persuaded to go to war in the Holy Cause.

Bonding through Bloodshed

A US television documentary programme was made about the American Vietnam veterans. For the last twenty five years, they have met together twice a year. At their meetings they sing songs together about love, and the spirit of peace between all men. Somehow as young men aged 19, 20, 21, they had physically survived the grotesque horrors of that desperate war. They remained deeply psychologically scarred by their memories of the grotesque moments of human suffering they had witnessed: the smell of burning flesh, screaming children, wounded weeping comrades approaching death. Most of all, they have been enduringly affected by the memories of their lost comrades in arms. These veterans had become an intense emotional brotherhood.

The emotional and psychological ties that build up between heroes in war, are of a very special nature. War unites men in extreme ways. They share a brotherhood of belief in the cause for which they are fighting. Communism,

The Lost Patriarch

Nazism, Liberal Democracy, Radical Islam, a homeland for Palestine, a United Ireland. This common identification with the Cause, and the shared experience of terror and death, helps men let go of many of the tensions that otherwise keep then from getting close to each other. They build and share a common identity. Seeing a common enemy out there, brings them together ever closer to one another. This is a universal phenomenon of war: whatever the cause, whoever the enemy, men get closer to each other fighting against other men.

As they prepare for war, their preparations become more intense and challenging. Their training becomes more and more physically dangerous. But nothing prepares them for the actual hell of battle, and the reality that at any moment they could die a bloody and terrifying death, together. It is this sharing of the terrifying moments of death and battle, that forges an unbreakable bond of brotherhood between men at war. Men who train for battle and risk death together, are bonded by an intense cord of love for one another. They realise that their lives literally come to depend on the skill of their comrades. Consequently they develop a mutual intensity of attachment, that perhaps no other experience allows between men. When they lose a colleague alongside whom they fought in a trench, or with whom they flew a plane, they will weep uncontrollably as for a lost brother. This seems to be the greatest emotional paradox of war; by hating and killing other men, men come to love each other.

Stephen Duke

Male Brotherhood and Sport

When men take part actively in competitive sports, they express heroic themes: the challenge, danger, victory. In sporting team tasks, they compete with other men through co-operating with their own team men. This enables an intimate closeness with other men, which men are not normally allowed. For a long time in western cultures like our own, men have had an unease about closeness with each other. Sporting brotherhood, sharing the challenge together, has allowed them to experience a certain type of manly intimacy. In the pursuit of sporting excellence and victory over other men, men are permitted to bond in a loving mateship

When we attend a large sporting event with forty, fifty, sixty thousand people, the "spirit of the occasion" moves us. Irresistibly we are connected to a larger energy that we tune into that is all around us. The isolated individual male ego connects with a communal consciousness. We feel connected effortlessly, through taking part as an observer of a sporting event, to something immense and uplifting. Sport seems to have the power to activate an heroic spiritual energy in men, whether as direct participants or observers of the event. The magnificent, epic stadia we have built for great sporting events, have become cathedrals for the heroic male spirit in sport. To go there, is to become tuned into as a man the great celebration of the heroic male spirit that is all around us there. We can experience a "high" that can stay with us for several days afterwards. Men have

The Lost Patriarch

always been able to experience this kind of spirit, when they have joined together in immense numbers. Football, Motor Sport, Rugby, Cricket, Tennis, Basketball, Ice Hockey, Bull Fighting; they are all forms of gladiatorial combat, staged, witnessed and celebrated by the machsimo male spirit. Let's have more of it. Lots more; as an alternative to war!

The Cult of Cricketers

The great and beautiful game of cricket, (like many great sports) has created a supreme cult of manhood. It is both a highly competitive and sublimely aesthetic sport, with an immensely strong and living tradition. It enjoys a living historical connection, to the great heroes of the past and the sporting heroes of today. The great player-heroes of the past, are connected through an unbroken chain of male memory and sporting myth, to the male heroes of the present. Stories are told about the immense sporting deeds of the past: the magnificent hundreds they scored, the great victories fast bowlers set up, the sublime achievements of spin bowlers. Playing essentially the same game, with fundamentally the same rules and objectives, provides a living stream of brotherhood between the men of different times and us.

Tribes and WarGames

In contrast to the warm spirit of communal participation that a sporting crowd can experience, the spirit of Nationalism is born out of male tribal psychology. It belongs to ancient tribalism and the early times of patriarchy. It is

Stephen Duke

not a subject we seem keen to talk about, as pervading our enjoyment of sport. England against the All Blacks at rugby. England against Germany in football. India against Pakistan in cricket. Then the dark monster of our male tribal psychology can rear up its ugly head. Australia playing against England in the ashes series, and a man suddenly finds himself overcome by strangely powerful emotions, stirring in his heart, overwhelming his head. Hateful aggression, the search for dominance, victory over the other side the enemy, at almost any cost. It is an aspect of our past tribal psychology, that we want to keep locked away inside the evolutionary bin of human history. The desire for victory at sport over another nation, ignites out primeval male lust for conquest. We dress up this tribal psychology in the garb of national sport, containing it and somehow making it safer. The feelings that can overwhelm us, are primitive and belong to our past, when a man needed them to survive in a dangerous and uncertain world. They still live on in men, genetically and psychologically. They can become activated, just by tuning into our television to watch the big game. Underneath the game, it can still be a battle of the tribes. Tribes playing each other at games however, means that tribes are much less likely to go to war. At a primal level of our masculine psychology, sport and games are a substitute psychological release for our warfaring male instincts

Games = Warfare with Different Rules

Most sports seem to have cheats, but not all sportsmen cheat.

The Lost Patriarch

When the rules are broken the game is no longer a game. Games depend on rules, and these rules are necessary to give a boundary to our wilder, amoral, primitiveness that wants to dominate at all costs. When rules are broken in sport, emotions can get very worked up. The lines between war and sport can be very thin dividing lines, especially when rules breakdown and players cheat. Both on and off the field, sport disintegrates into violence. Violent and fatal clashes at club level have occurred in football over the last few years. Violence seems to surround football at club and international level. Violent conflict has regularly now entered the streets around certain international fixtures.

There is one international rugby team, whose "sporting" strategy for some years, was clearly to try and illegally injure as many of the opposing team as possible. The first twenty minutes of their "game" looked less like a ball sport than blood sports. Their intention was to use every illegal physical means, to cripple the opposing team's best players and get them off the sporting field. By reducing their opponent's superior skill advantage in this way, they believed they could then go on to win the game. This kind of planned, strategic violence in sport erodes the thin boundaries between a hard contact sport and violent warfare.

Boxing is a brutal, violent, dangerous sport men still play and watch. Depending on the skill of the participants, it can range from being a hand to hand battle of brutal force between two fearless male opponents, or an art form. For most of the men who do it, it is 80% the former and 20%

Stephen Duke

the latter. The great boxer and ring dancer Mohammed Ali did the art form: the other American, Mike Tyson seemed to do more of the battle of brute force. For many men (and women) it is compelling to watch. It is the nearest sport we have in our culture to the gladiatorial combat of the ancient roman arena. We have thrown away the swords and put on gloves. Boxers regularly get serious head and brain injuries and occasionally die. Only a hundred years ago, bare knuckle fighting was a major spectator and gambling sport.

It seems reasonable to say that many young men, and I emphasise the word young, are keen to "go to war." This keenness is an urgent need to release and express the archetypal warrior instinct, that underneath remains as powerfully active in our male psyche, as it was 100,000 years ago. Then it served an essential purpose; physical survival on the killing fields of the hunt. It seems that we cannot just suddenly turn off a mechanism psycho-genetically encoded into us. Nature and evolution works at a much slower pace than that.

However in the future world of post patriarchy we must ask ourselves a fundamental question, as important to our survival now as killing has been in the past. Does the killer instinct serve as a survival purpose in our post patriarchal world? Or does it just make the world a more dangerous place and therefore our survival less certain? I believe that each individual man has an urgent priority. He needs to find a way to tap into the fearsome energy of the hero-warrior; then he must learn how to use that energy

The Lost Patriarch

creatively, rather than destructively. To harness it to an activity, sport or cause that keeps it safe and directed, and under his control. If harnessed and controlled, as in the martial arts of the East, it promotes physical, mental and spiritual development of the highest level.

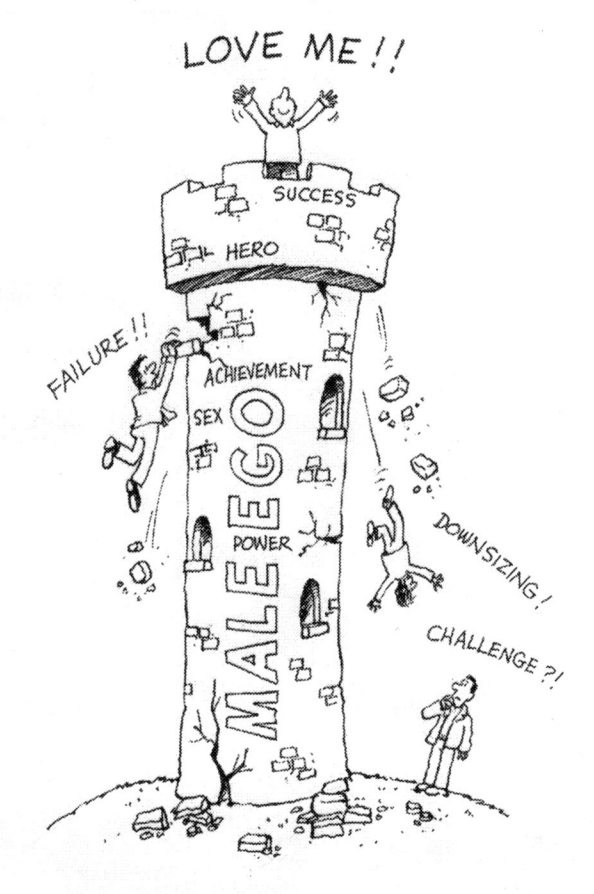

THE FRAGILE TOWER

Stephen Duke

On the Patriarchal Psychology of Winning,

Winning at sport is based on the warrior psychology of conquest. Beat the opposition, destroy the enemy, inflict defeat upon them. One victory is not enough. In a competition, we need to inflict defeat after defeat upon all the enemies we can find. Only then when all the enemies have been defeated, do we win the ultimate victory and receive the ultimate honour: being called Champions of the World!

There are other wars to fight, other honours to seek out. More noble wars and compassion driven victories: to defeat the global epidemic of Aids, or give every child on the planet clean water to drink, or build a school in every village in the world. Men must embrace the truth about themselves. **At this moment in their evolutionary psychology, they are a contradictory mixture of the primitive and the compassionate, the instinctive and the rational, the warrior and the poet, the patriarchal and the post patriarchal.**

All men carry around deep inside them, a dark shadow of racist fear. This shadow can be triggered quite suddenly by events such as: fear of invasive overcrowding and immigration, defeat at national sports, coming second, national propaganda, heterosexual rivalry. We can all experience the feelings quite suddenly, and be shocked by how overwhelming they can become. They are the dark or shadow side of the warrior archetype. The energy of this warrior/hero archetype, is still very much at the centre of our masculine psychological life.

*The future of Mankind depends on each individual man,
evolving beyond this and to making the
GLOBAL CONNECTION.
To do this we have to embrace and celebrate the
new reality of
ONE WORLD OF MANY NATIONS*

Male Portraits: "Sammy The Tattoo"

Sammy is the original Hardman. Physically abused from a young age by his alcoholic step father, (Sammy's own father abandoned the family, when Sammy was just three months old), he was also routinely severely bullied by his two older brothers. Sammy's physical hardness and emotional imbalance, was forged in an abusively rigorous "family school " of toughness. Sammy learned at a young age, to fight his way through a childhood, where respect was based on fear, cruelty and a sadistic use of male power. Sammy's earliest memories are of a household, where violence was an everyday occurrence. He has no memories of being nurtured. For him, authority has always been experienced as dangerous, over controlling and associated with painful conflict. The sense of right from wrong has always been confused in his emerging male psyche.

Stephen Duke

In addition to his emotional and physical disadvantages, Sammy was born severely dyslexic. He was still illiterate when he dropped out of main stream school, at the age of 13. His learning having been severely handicapped by his dyslexia, he was expelled from two senior schools, for his uncontrollable behaviour in class and an inability to respond to baseline discipline. Infused with greater and greater levels of testosterone, his powerful brawny physique grew stronger by the day The education system finally gave up on him, when one year later, he head butted his teacher of religious studies, in the Special Education Unit to which in desperation he had been sent.

Sammy's real talent had always been for oppositional behaviour. This graduated into delinquency and crime as he grew older. His criminal apprenticeship began in the street gangs of the Big City, to which he naturally graduated from school. At sixteen he was an antisocial veteran of car theft, assault, small time burglary, and drug dealing on an increasing scale. Sammy's manhood initiation had been a 14 hour tattoo ceremony, in which he had his hands, arms, chest, back and shaven head, sculptured with images of the great pagan warrior heroes. He and his friends then stole a Mercedes open top, and embarked on a drug crazed crime spree for the next three days. By the age of nineteen, Sammy had begun his first prison sentence; a little six month stretch for grievous bodily harm, with a suspicion of racial motivation behind it. The judge however, had looked upon him with clemency, seeing a young man still with the potential *for "social rehabilitation and moral redemption." Sammy however, graduated from prison, with the consciousness of a fully decorated criminal, intent upon greater and greater achievements within his chosen amoral career. Greater deeds of darkness will lie ahead of him............*

CHAPTER 7:
"The New Male Life Cycle"

The Changing Story of the New Male Life Cycle

There is a natural shape to the story of a man's life, and his changing boyhood, masculinity and manhood. It evolves and emerges slowly as a physical, emotional, sexual, spiritual and heroic narrative passing through its various stages. Whilst it is happening to him, he is so subjectively entangled within its intense dramas, that it can be difficult if not impossible for him to see a shape or meaning to it all. This life perspective can only come with the aging process; the growing up over time and the perspective of distance from what he once was. With change through living time, comes some self knowledge, and an emerging awareness of the pattern of his male life story. For many thousands of years, this male life cycle has been essentially the same. Although men have lived in widely different cultures for many thousands of years, the fundamental and important moments in the narrative of manhood have been the same. Now the male life cycle is suddenly changing in important and fundamental ways.

Certain key events are still an essential part of this male story: attachment to his mother and then separation from her, and re-attachment to another woman. Attachment to *father as his son, and then deeper attachment to him in adolescence as man to man. Discovering how to be a hero of achievement through sport and work. Becoming a sexual hero and a lover. Forming bonds with other boys and then with other men. Becoming a father, and exploring the role of provider, that comes with making his own family. These are the timeless changes that have been at the centre of the male story for many thousands of years. Nowadays, new extra challenges are being written into the story. None of the timeless challenges are being left out, but new ones are being added. In post patriarchy, there is an earthquake of change, now shifting the basic ground plan of what makes up the male life story.*

As every new decade of post patriarchy arrives, living as a man through the new male life cycle is becoming more and more complex and challenging. For example, fathers now have to do the school run before going off to work. Then they have to come home and supervise homework, or cook the supper three days or four a week. They are expected to be gardeners and cooks, providers and nurturers, DIY experts, executives and nappy changers. They still have the traditional emotional responsibility, father to son, of bonding in a manly masculine way, through sport and physical challenges. Now they are also expected to teach their sons how to be tender, more unselfish and how and to open up to their emotions. They are expected to become hero-achievers in their twenties at work. And at the same time, they have to become accustomed to work for women bosses in the work place. They have to find a way to be co-equal with their woman partner, in achievement, emotionally, sexually and within the home. Taken all in all, the new male life cycle, brings ever more complex challenges to the emerging psychology of the post patriarchal male.

Half of all men, now create a family and then lose it through a divorce. The lifecycle decades of the thirties and forties, are most commonly the battleground for this arduous part of the new male life cycle story. Most men then re-marry or form a new partnership and another kind of family, often mixing their own and their new partner's children together. This is a vast and largely unexplored emotional territory in the life story of manhood.

In addition, work and career are no longer an unchanging certainty in the new male lifecycle. Typically, it now involves several big changes and upheavals, caused by redundancy and re-training. Men are getting used to being with one company or organisation for 10 or 15 years, being made redundant, retraining and then starting a new professional venture somewhere else. Increasingly a man will go on to have a third or even fourth career, during his working lifetime. A man often struggles hard to achieve in one career, only then to experience at some point burnout and breakdown. Others give their best and most creative and hardworking years, only then to be kicked out onto the scrap heap, by the organisation to whom they have been unflinchingly loyal.

More and more men re-train, and start entirely new careers in their thirties and forties.

In mid-life, a man begins to experience a sense of his mortality. Bones crunch, bodies take longer to heal, friends get sick, even die. By his thirties, he is no longer the immortal "master of the universe ", he believed himself to be in his mid and late twenties. Eventually, somewhere in his forties he falls into what is called the mid life crisis. This "crisis" is in fact, a hugely creative life transition, and an opportunity for the fragile male ego to break up, change and grow. Glimpsing his own limitations of selfhood, a man has the opportunity to connect with something much larger around and inside himself. This puts him on a spiritual path that he can either embrace or push away.

Stage 1: Infant Bonding with Mother AND Father

Recently an England cricket captain left the ground during a crucial Test match, to be present at and witness the birth of his new baby daughter. The year before, another England sportsman, a rugby player, flew all the way home from Australia to see his unwell pregnant wife, during a World Cup tournament. These actions confirm the fundamental shifts in manhood, and the post patriarch's new and intense involvement in nurturing.

Men are taking on new responsibilities as partners and fathers. They are bonding with their partner and child, during pregnancy, at birth, and from the earliest moments of early childcare. In the past, in patriarchy, pregnancy, childbirth and the early infant years, were very much a world for *women and children. Men were excluded from them. The patriarchal fathers picked up and cuddled their babies and then handed them back to their mothers. Men did not try to learn the complex skills of nurturing childcare. They saw their babies and wives at the weekend, in between other life priorities: work, achievement, career, sport; babies and young kids did pretty poorly on the contact–nurture time with their dads. Not anymore. Now it is ALL CHANGE! In post-patriarchy, one of the biggest, perhaps the biggest change in the lives of men is to do with:*

CONTACT TIME
NURTURE TIME
EMOTIONAL BONDING
FATHER CHILD ATTACHMENT
PSYCHOLOGY

Human beings bond through contact. When psychologists first started to observe and describe the behaviours that led to bonding between parents and children, it was the 1950's. The 1950's was the last true decade of Patriarchy in western culture. Millions of men had returned home from the war, as hero warriors. (Women had experienced a temporary liberation during the war labour market. Then they had gone out to work in their many millions and kept the country going). Now, they briefly returned to the home and kitchen. They started the "baby boom" and become full time nurturers and homemakers again. The child psychologists were trying to find out more about how human beings

Stephen Duke

become psychologically attached during infancy. They found themselves studying the old patriarchal family, and so observed mothers and babies, infants and young children. The fathers were at work, happily being providers for their home and family. Because the fathers were absent so much of the family time, they were considered peripheral to the intense nurture, care and play that was going on at home between the rest of the family. Psychologists developed the theory that children bonded first to mothers. Father /child attachment was hardly studied, if at all. The theory of attachment emerged that described mothers as the **primary attachment figure.** This patriarchal theory of parent child attachment still operates today. It has not been modified in any significant way, to reflect the enormous changes in family organisation and structure, that have been happening over the last forty years. It continues to influence employers, schools, the legal system, families themselves. Interestingly films and TV dramas do show the true changes in father child attachment in their storymaking and storytelling.

Feminism has blown away patriarchy, and with it goes the idea that women stay at home and look after babies all the time. With it went the idea that men go out to work all the time, and don't get involved in looking after children. Over the last forty years, men have gradually become introduced to the richly intimate exchanges and sustained loving contact, which forms the intimate care of babies and infants. Along with the first principle of post patriarchy: **women go out more to work to achieve**

The Lost Patriarch

and provide, *is the equally important second principle;* **men stay more at home and learn how to nurture.** *With this fundamental change, out goes the old idea that women and mothers are the primary attachment figure for their children. This theory belonged to patriarchy. It implies that fathers are emotionally peripheral to the early bonding process, between child and parent. In post patriarchy, the intimate ongoing contact of fathers with their babies, infants and young children, results in a fundamental shift in a new model of the family as a psychological system.* **With co-equality among couples, comes co-attachment between children and their two parents.**

This has enormous emotional fallout to newly forming families, and then to families who later fall apart. As men routinely change nappies, share sleepless nights of bottle feeding with ravenous babies, touch, stroke, cuddle, coo-coo and bathe their soft and demanding infants, and perform as playful partners to their young children, a new psychology of childhood is starting to emerge. One consequence is that in families where the co-equal couple share the early care of their child, the new male life cycle begins with a young boy enjoying close, warm, sustained and intimate bonding with both their father **and** *mother. This new intimacy contact of bonding, has the potential to change the relationship between fathers and sons and fathers and daughters forever.*

There is a potential downside to this. The emotional distress and overpowering grief that fathers now feel when families fall apart, and they become separated from their children on a daily basis, is in direct proportion to the new **intensity of attachment** *they have formed through their hands on immersion in childcare.*

Stage 2: Heroes and Boys' Groups

All young boys are natural storymakers. Hero play is at the centre of a young boy's world. It is so important at this age, (2-7 years old), that it is clearly fundamental to the second step in the male life cycle. For the first time, a young boy has a sense of his own imaginative authority over the world around him. Hero play starts with small toys and develops into "real" hero play with other boys in hero dramas. At the centre of this play, is storymaking. This making up and performing of hero stories in a young boy's play, sets out the major life themes for the next three decades of male psychology and the male life cycle. It places ways of becoming a hero, at the very epicentre of a young boy's psychology. Exploring the hero quest in some emotionally active way, enables a young boy to begin the epic journey, into and through his manhood. He does this by playing out the thrilling emotions associated with adventure, confrontation, danger, exploration, discovery, conquest and victory. These archetypal themes of the hero later become translated into "real" life as: male identity, pursuing aims, setting a challenging target, competition, study, ambition, achievement. As well as central to his development of language and thinking, this stage is a laboratory in which he can develop his emerging male identity.

As they learn how to play interactively with one another, boys form their first male groups. Along with this interactive play, comes the discovery of something fundamental about themselves and each other: their potential for cruelty and their capacity to inflict pain on each other. Until now the male life cycle has been a protective safe zone. It has been about experiencing care, nurture and bonding with mother and father. Joining the boys' group, reveals something entirely different about life and being a boy. Male bonding between peers. Belonging to a boys' group releases for the first time, the competitive warrior instincts and their darker patterns of behaviour. Along with the creative thrill of discovering how to play heroes together, comes the reality of dominance, power, cruelty and the need to belong. Overweight boys get called "fatty" and are bullied. Pretty boys get called "girlie" and are teased and hit. Whose "in" and whose "out", becomes important for the first time. Inclusion and exclusion to and from the male group, are exciting and anxious experiences in equal measure. All this confirms the growing sense of a masculine identity in this second stage of the new male life cycle.

The young boy also needs to prove himself in the group, to be a hero of some worth, in order to win the respect of other boys. This prevents him from becoming the victim of further teasing and bullying. In this way, becoming a respected, worthy member of the young boys' group, is a very early **ritual of initiation** into maleness and some degree of "toughness" essential for masculinity. This toughness is defined by the ability to defend yourself from the cruelty of other boys, to stand up for yourself and not become a victim of others in life.

Already quite a journey has been made in the new male life cycle. A boy has travelled through babyhood and infancy, receiving the nurturing care of father and mother, and developed safe, intense and secure co-equal attachments. Then he has become the hero in his play, both alone and with other boys. Next he has entered the world of male bonding through joining the boy's group, and discovered the competition and toughness, necessary to affirm his growing masculine identity. What next?

First Encounters with the Love Goddess

Miss Little was the first woman to show me or reveal to me, that there was even more to my love life, than mother love. She was a trainee teacher who came to our school when I was eight. Small, brunette and astonishingly pretty, she awoke something in me that has stayed awake ever since. She switched on in me, a longing I had never previously experienced. I remember having dreams about her. Together we celebrated our pre-pubertal enchantment. Something was there stirring, which I had never known before. The ache that I experienced in her presence, was not an explicitly erotic desire. Nevertheless, it was something more than the longing for nurture, safety and trust that infused a young boy's feelings for closeness and intimacy with mother.

When I was nine and a half, I fell in love for the first time; with Beautiful, Blond Sally. Sally was golden haired, astonishingly beautiful and kind. Above all else, it was her warmth and softness which drew me towards her. I developed an insatiable appetite for her company. I wanted to be with her, alongside her, to sleep in her house with her, to be in her company all the time. She was my first falling-in-love experience. It seemed a possibility this time that something could happen between us. For a start, Sally was the same age as me. Looking back, the intensity of my desire for her frightened her away. She ran away and got her parents to ban me from the house!

Stage 3: Adolescence and Puberty

The previous years have been years of "switching on" the masculine identity in boys. Now a boy suddenly encounters a momentous change in himself. His emerging sexuality seeks greater and greater contact and intimacy with the love goddess, who is already an emotionally liberated, independent thinking female focussed on her own goals and achievements in the world.

It is the explosion of hormones and sexual growth, that makes it possible to have sex with the love goddess, with whom young boys are already "falling-in-love." There are two sex gods in the male, (Rampant Sex God and Love Prince). It is the beginnings of the encounter with the Love Goddess/liberated young female, which begins a boy's **healthy growing de-tachment** *from his mother.*

Stephen Duke

Manmaking in Post Patriarchy

I remember the first time a mother brought her young pubertal son to see me for therapy. The 11 year old male sat there silent and withdrawn, with a bored look spread across his sullen, angry face. "I don't know what has happened to him " she complained to me. "We have got on so well together since his father left five years ago; just the two of us together; our own close loving little family. But now we argue all the time and he won't do anything I ask him to do. He runs away to his room, swears at me all the time. He gets so angry that he even smashes the place up."

Try as she might, the post feminist female, (liberated powergirl and single parent that she may have become), cannot provide **fathering** *in his emerging adolescence to her pubescent son. What was clear about the small family I was seeing, was that something profound and natural was unfolding inside the boy's head and heart; and lower down in his body. It was the dynamic of the third stage of the male life cycle change, happening in a mother's single parent post patriarchal family. When puberty starts, it is triggered by a huge increase in growth and sex hormones. A boy has a transforming experience of intense bodily changes. He starts to look and feel like a young man. At the same time, an intense psychological process also occurs. There is instinctive drive to begin to demand greater freedom, independence, and start a process of parent child separation that will eventually end in leaving home. Puberty starts all of this in an active way. Boys start to search for a way to* *become men. The continual presence of a father or father figure, means a triangle of family love in which the adolescent boy does not feel too emotionally and sexually crowded. Mother son love, without the empowering combination of father son love, suffocates the independence seeking young male, wanting to identify more and more with the world of male teenagers and manhood. To begin his search, he has to find a way of feeling more separate from mother. Like the boy who was sitting in front of me, looking angry and sullen, this can be hard to do with no man around. Without a father around to give them that extra push, they will have to struggle that much harder to "get away". Boys beginning their psychological adolescence, need a father to help them in very practical ways in their quest towards manhood. The more or less constant presence of a father is crucial in giving praise and recognition of their male achievements. When they get a place on the football or rugby team; score a goal or a try; receive an end of season medal for most improved player; pass a music exam or get excellent for their end of term report. There is also the special bonding that comes from spending "boys time" with each other. Playing sport on the lawn together: seeing who is the fastest swimmer in the pool: testing their strength against each other in an arm wrestle, watching a match on television, together. All of these experiences strengthen male intimacy, deepen the father son attachment, and confirm a* **son's emerging identification with manhood.**

The re-organisation of family structure and patterns in so many post patriarchal families; the break-up of so many families; the separation for much of the time of divorced sons and their fathers; or the complete absence of fathers in so many families, can result in only one outcome for male adolescence. In the new male life cycle, **adolescence is becoming more difficult to negotiate.**

Male Adolescence: "The Long In-Between "

During most of human history there was no such thing as male **adolescence**, or teenage growing up.

Boys became men OVERNIGHT!!

In every tribe, in every culture, this was done by separating them first from their mothers and the rest of the family. Around the age of puberty, they were taken away by the men, and made a man. This was done using lots of different methods. There was a common theme to all the male rites of passage. They were brutal, beautiful, terrifying, transformational and final. Boys were tattooed, beaten, given hallucinogenic drugs, had their heads shaved, noses and bodies pierced (without anaesthetic), abandoned and left alone terrified on a mountainside overnight or for longer. They were then further initiated by being told secret, heroic stories of manhood. After all of this there was no going back. Manhood had arrived, with a short and shocking explosion of consciousness. Boyhood had gone forever. Unlike today and the long in between (childhood and manhood), adolescence is full of uncertainty and

The Lost Patriarch

confusion. In traditional male rites of passage, you knew who you were, and what you were and what the rest of your life was going to be about: being a man.

For most of human time, and even now in many cultures, a young male's sexual maturation is celebrated with a pagan simplicity and power. In rural Italy, a pubescent son is taken into the woods by his father. His mother accompanies them. The son is stripped naked, and his genitals ritualistically rubbed against the bark of a young sapling tree. The symbolism in this simple but powerfully transforming event, changes the young boy's psychology for ever. It recognises, affirms, honours and celebrates his emergent sexuality, within the wide context of Nature and Manhood.

These male rites of male passage have one by one all but disappeared. They are disowned by a civilised culture, as belonging to a primitive and pagan past. The journey to manhood in a post patriarchy is becoming harder and harder to make. The shock and suddenness of the rite of passage had many advantages. Suddenly and explosively you became a man, recognised by the other men as such, and you felt good about it. A boy's manhood psychology had been grown up overnight. The number one masculine archetype, how to be a hero, could easily find its natural expression. The contrast with what we have now is immense; teenage angst, identity confusion and crisis, ongoing battles with authority, the emotional struggle to get away from mother and frequently the unfulfilled longing for an absent father.

And all of this in a prolonged enduring struggle lasting eight to ten years.

In the world of today and the future, the change from boy to man, means negotiating an ever longer and more complicated transition. The society of post patriarchy no longer knows when or how to make boys into men. The journey through these years grows more and more of a struggle for the male adolescent. Nature still gives him at puberty, the sexual and physical drive for freedom and manhood, all in a rush. But he spends his adolescence in years of conflict, at home, school and with wider authority, wrestling his confused search for identity and independence from people. It cannot be handed over to him, in the straightforward simplicity of old.

To many adolescents, the final stage of independence gaining, can prove itself too difficult. They remain stalled and stuck, frozen in the oncoming headlights of manhood. Separation from home is delayed. The step off into manhood, or at least the search for it, is postponed later and later. Fathers and sons need each other more and more at this time. The caring father, nurtures his son and recognises his physical and psychological changes.

The story of the small fatherless family who came to see me for their consultation, demonstrates to me how difficult it can now be, for sons to get manmaking time with fathers. Half of all families now end up in divorce and break-up. This enforced separation, can be a devastating interruption to fathers and sons, especially if it happens between the *age of 11-18. 50% of fathers then lose regular contact with their children, within the first two years of family break-up and divorce. In those families that do stay together, fathers and sons struggle to see more of one another. We now live in an Overwork culture, where men are driven to work longer and longer hours away from their families; but seeking more nurturing contact with them. Research clearly shows that more fathers want to reduce their time at work, and increase their time at home with their families and children.*

Now 40% of all children born in the UK, are born to families whose parents are not married. Many of these couples will break-up, and fathers cut-off contact all together with their sons. All of these factors make the crucial role that fathers can play in the manmaking initiation of their sons, less likely to happen. A father is the best person to play this initiator role, because of the intense and positive **male identification** *that naturally exists from son to father and father to son. The son's image of himself in doing worthy masculine things, and the reinforcement of his male identity, can best come about through this father son psychological exchange. The son is immensely hungry for the father's recognition and approval. He cannot get enough of it. Having enough, enables his psychological emergence through what we call adolescence, into manhood. Not enough of it, leaves disappointment, confusion rejection and anger. Manmaking has always been a vital and dramatic event in the story of the* male life cycle. In the new male life cycle, men and fathers have to rediscover its importance.

The single mother who brought her son to see me, said she was unhappy about her lack of control over him. She was also emotionally distressed, because she felt a deepening sense of him pushing her away. She felt pain at the loss of their deep emotional intimacy, which they had enjoyed together as a single parent, mother/son family. This was a healthy process for him, although a painful one for her. The son needs to push his mother away in order to free the path to manhood that she blocks for him. In the psychological business of manmaking, fathers guide the way to manhood, mothers block it.

The 3 stages of the Long In-Between: (A pocket guide for fathers and sons)

For those lucky fathers who are in close contact with their sons, there are important things for them to know and understand about their sons. The long in-between of adolescence has become so expanded in our post patriarchy, that we have to divide it into 3 sections: **early, mid and late.**

STAGE ONE (puberty to 14 years old)

In the early adolescence stage (puberty normally happens as early as 10 as late as 14 years old), a boy has his childhood shattered by sex and growth. Seminal emissions confuse him in his bed at night and he masturbates during the day. His body suddenly grows at a rate he has never

The Lost Patriarch

experienced before. He feels himself detaching from the blissful comfort and safety of childhood, and rocketing off into the unknown vastness of being a teenager. This early first stage of adolescence is a period of radical change and adjustment, for sons, fathers and families. During this early explosive period of change, the nurturing father needs to provide reassurance, security and a strong, calm presence. In this early stage, the son has to be allowed to go off into his own psychological territory and explore within and without. He has to discover a relationship with his new sexuality and the female gender. The good father respects this need for personal action, but is also present to give advice and recognition when his son asks for it. At some point, fathers and sons need close heart to heart talks, about the practical and emotional aspects of sex and relationships with girls. In this early stage when everything is still so unfamiliar and still a bit shocking, a teenage son can lose confidence, struggle with his self esteem, become socially withdrawn, have wide mood swings and feel isolated. This is all normal early teenage behaviour. The teenage son is moving into a new and strange world; in one day he can be companionable and close with his family, and then become brash, overbearing and confrontational. On another day, he may be vulnerable, withdrawn, uncommunicative and unhappy.

STAGE TWO (14-17 years old)

During the long in between of adolescence, stage two is the experimentation-conflict stage. Punks, Goths, retro Hippies, Garage, Skins, Hoodies, Chavs, all offer a radically different image and lifestyle to the older generation. The son is seriously into his own thing. He is enjoying his own emerging identity and independent sense of self. At the same time as doing his own thing, he is needing to do it in secret, alone and with his own closely knit group of friends. This stage is about getting into himself in a serious way. This is a time of really contradictory messages from son to father. Underneath the son's new idealism, self-centredness and rebelliousness, he is longing for recognition and approval from his father. He wants more and more to do things in his own way, and he wants father to accept, admire and praise what he is doing. This can be hard for a father, when he sees him making some of the mistakes he made: not studying, not working hard enough, being anti-everything, drinking too much, even experimenting with drugs. One father came to see me, complaining of his son's disobedience and unreasonable behaviour. It turned out that the father had made a lot of mistakes himself, during his own teenage years. He had dropped out of school and done drugs for a couple of years. His relationship with his own father had broken down during this period, when he was 15-16 years old. His own father had then died suddenly, before they had been able to get back together and become emotionally close again. Now in his own role as a father, he was finding it too difficult to give away his protective concern for his own teenage son. He dreaded that his own son would rebel, and that he would fail as a father. This made him emotionally possessive and too controlling with

The Lost Patriarch

his son. His son felt the need to push harder and harder against his father and was in danger of becoming a self destructive rebel. So the very thing the father feared most, he was in danger of bringing about!

Somehow a father needs to keep a creative dialogue going between himself and his son, during this crucial stage two of adolescence. Sharing learning and homework together, playing a sport together, watching his son playing sport, watching a movie together, chatting to him about a book he is reading; anything that is still keeping you in touch with one another. The key thing is to both share your similar interests, and accept the differences between you. There will also be a need to **negotiate** together about rules of living inside and outside the home. This is normal, creative and life affirming. Your son needs to begin to believe and feel that he is starting to take a more adult ownership of the lifestyle rules that govern his new life. He cannot get to stage three of adolescence, (the leaving home stage), unless he has started this process of challenging and taking control of his life in a more active way. Your skill as a father now, is in giving him an increasing sense of control over his own life, while still living in and sharing the family home together. Give him a key to the door of the home, and take a leap of trust that goes with it.

Gradually fathers need to give away their protective control of their little boy, now growing into a young man. The danger at this time, is for communication to break down between father and son over the rules of living. Sons *need to challenge fathers, and some conflict is inevitable and healthy. It allows the son to flex the psychological muscles of his emerging manhood. A son's view of the world and his intense emotions about the events in it, are new and strongly felt. Fathers must understand and respect the precious and newly emerging identity of their son during this time. It is a brief and passing stage, and the loving skilful father is able to accompany his son through it, with their emotional closeness remaining intact between them.*

STAGE THREE (17-20 years old)

Teenagers enter stage three of adolescence, with a stronger sense of themselves confirmed, as to who they are and what they want to be. They have been growing into themselves for several years now as a young person. They have a clearer sense of their identity and a growing sense of control over their own lives. In the new male life cycle, this is the time when a male teenager enters his manhood. At seventeen, eighteen, nineteen, twenty, he is introduced as a young man. A number of key events happen during this late adolescent stage. Although still living at home, he takes more and more **decisions on his own.** *A young man aged seventeen came to see me. He was dealing with the usual issues at home between himself and his parents: conflict over house rules, study, drinking, earning money. The one thing that was clear for him, was that he wanted to make up his own mind about his future plans. He had decided to make a big change in his studies, and move more towards arts subjects (film studies, media etc.) This* *was in contrast to his two parents, with whom he was still living. They were doctors and scientists. He told me that he was determined to make up his own mind, about his own future life plans. He had understood that he was going to have to live his life in his own way and for himself. He dreaded the confrontation with his parents and their family script. This said: "science is good; arts are bad and unsafe as an occupation." His parents joined us for a session of "manmaking". They understood that they could not live his life for him, and had been deliberately and unconsciously, influencing him to go against his natural artistic interests. This was big stuff in the teenager manmaking stakes.*

The next key manmaking event at this third stage, is the leaving school and going to work, college or university event. Half of young men leave school and go to work; the other half go into professional training at college and university. Either way the business of school is over, and the world of work is beginning. Changing from teenage schoolboy to young man at work, is probably now the most significant rite of passage left in our industrial culture. To the 50% who do it, it represents a huge psychological and lifestyle event. It happens suddenly. Many young men, then enter a professional skills training programme that lasts three four or more years. The rest join the labour force. They work alongside other older men and are treated as one of them by their employers. They earn a "man's wage". Nearly all young men who go out to work at this stage, now live at home for a further period but pay for their keep.

At the same time, a young man now seeks more and more adult adventure and excitement. Young men have always sought out adventure and our time is no exception. Bungee jumping, parachuting, binge drinking, car racing, motor biking, fighting, sexual promiscuity, gambling, experimenting with drugs, musicmaking, hero sports; these are just a few of the ways in which young men initiate themselves further into manhood. This is because our culture lets them down on the initiation stakes. They now have to do it for themselves and to each other. Becoming a young man at work, also means becoming a serious young man at play.

There is still a final step-off into the uncertain territory of manhood in our new post patriarchy: leaving home. Sooner or later it has to be done. The academic young men do it by going off to college and university. The rest set up home with each other, in small house share groups of three or four. A small number set up home straight away with a woman. However it is done, it cuts the final umbilical chord with mother home and her safe, nurturing charms. It has taken 10 years to explore and achieve full male independence. Adolescence, the long in between, is now over. Standing in front of the mirror in his new rented flat or house, the former confused, angst ridden, spotty male teenager, can recognise himself for what finally he has now become; a young man.

(A Teenage Afterthought: Suicide by Cop and the case of alienated hero)

Do you remember the story of Columbine? Columbine is a small town of several thousand people high up in the Rockies in America. It was formerly a mining settlement where 19th century men, could be old fashioned heroes and seek their fortune by mining for gold and precious metals. In the year 2000, two male teenagers from the local high school, planned and carried out a murderous and terrifying shooting attack on their fellow school pupils. They shot **dead** twelve fellow school children and a male teacher. Whilst committing this act of mass murder, they were not under the influence of drugs or alcohol. Investigations discovered that the attack had been meticulously planned over the previous weeks and months. What is the psychopathology of male teenagers who commit such gross acts of murderous violence? How do they think and feel themselves, into the state of action that results in such behaviour? What went gone wrong in their manmaking process?

The obvious place to start to look for an answer, is their relationship with authority. Boys need fathers in the manmaking journey. For the son, the father is so often where male feelings about authority really take hold. Males work out much of their learning and attitude formation towards authority, with and though their fathers. There is a tension there from the start. When we begin our childhood with a positive father son relationship, authority becomes recognised, respected and understood by us through nurturing attachment. The bullying father uses too much *fear. At the time of the event, the horror was widespread and psychological theories to explain it abounded: separation from a natural father through abandonment, family break-up or divorce? Living with an over achieving, neglectful father who is absent to his son's emotional needs through over commitment to work? Confused, unresolved attitudes towards authority in a conflict ridden step-family? The final theory was of the cruel father who over controls, beats and physically abuses his son. The abusing father conveys the image of authority as dark, fearsome, cruel, remote; above all something to be resisted and ultimately fought against. This is all in contrast to the positive image of authority as strong but also safe, fair, protective, reasonable, restrained and in control.*

For whatever of combination of these or other causes, the son's image of authority may can be one of fear, abuse, neglect; a dark power to be resisted or fought against by the time he reaches the crucial age of puberty. Puberty usually coincides with a transfer to senior school. If a teenage male does not have an attachment to a positive male figure by then, he can be dynamite waiting to explode! Extraverts will tend to attack and destroy what is around them: introverts will damage themselves with drugs and self harm. The adolescent male discovers himself, through more and more daring exploration of what is around him. His respect for and attachment to his male authority figure, who slowly coaches and guides him through this experimentation, protects him from too dangerous extremes. If there is no father to whom

The Lost Patriarch

he is attached at home, a male teenager in his search for selfhood and young heroism, will take on the rebel identity in some way. He angrily **dis-identifies** *with authority at school. He sees it as something to be attacked constantly, destroyed if possible. It is a battle to fight, a war to be won, a glorious anti-victory to be gained. Psychologically he becomes* **anti**-*social, other than attached to his own excluding peer group. He jealously wants to attack and destroy, what he sees others around him enjoying, and which he himself cannot have. This is the profile of the angry rebel, who* (**with a gun in his hand**) *can do murderous things.*

To fully understand the disturbed male mindset, that plans and carries out a mass murder of other teenagers and teachers, we have to go further. From non attachment to a positive father or father figure, emerges an identity as the anti social rebel warrior, against school and authority. In addition, we have to consider his wider relationship with the community. He is not a member of the football squad or acting group or school choir, or any socially approved activity; so he has to become an anti-achiever. His raw talents are frustrated, and his male ego can grow only though negative acts in the role of anti-social rebel.

The final step this highly disturbed teenager takes into psychological and moral oblivion, is to challenge the ultimate figures of authority: the law enforcers of the police. In shooting to death their happily socialised peers, they also get to play the role of the ultimate **warrior anti-hero**. *The* male psyche is hungry with hero, especially in its youth. For these few deeply alienated teenagers, they also die their own perversely heroic suicide death, shot by the adult male figures they have grown to hate and fear; other men.

Stage Four: Master of the Universe or Metrosexual Male?

For a short magnificent period in his twenties, a young man can still believe himself to be a master of the universe. In his physical prime and fresh for life, he has not yet been hit by any of life's shocks. For a few brief years in his early to mid twenties, anything seems possible for him. At work, on the sporting field, between the sheets, in the bars and clubs, a young men flexes his muscles in every way he can. We call it the arrogance of youth. But compared to what is soon to come in the new male life cycle, it enables a young man to be an old fashioned hero for an all too short period. He can be self centred, driven by his unique goals and challenges; seeking and taking his own pleasures; trying to change the world in his own way. It is during these few brief years, that a young man may sometimes achieve his personal heights. At the age of 20, the footballer David Beckham scored a miraculous goal from the halfway line, instinctively lobbing the ball over the goal keeper's head when he saw him coming out of his goal. If he had been 25, would he have thought about it for a fraction of a second too long, and the opportunity passed him by? In their early twenties, young men are guided in their actions more often by their natural instincts, than their intellect or emotional

The Lost Patriarch

intelligence. It also enables them to feel less fear in the face of danger and threat. (This is the main reason why armies recruit young men in their late teens or early twenties, to do their killing deeds).

Showing a different kind of fearlessness, Richard Branson the entrepreneur started up his Virgin business empire in his early twenties. Bill Gates the Microsoft Zsar, is another of many examples of this original and creative period on a young man's life. Driven by an untamed self certainty, young men go off and do whatever they feel inclined or compelled to do in the world; win an Olympic gold medal, swim across the Atlantic ocean, get drunk four nights a week, or date three women in one day. It is the all too brief age of a glorious male selfishness, heroic achievement and exploration. The Rampant SexGod is often likely to go wild at this time. Overflowing with testosterone, young men are keen to be heroic sexual performers: adventure is the name of the sexual game. Q Magazine, Vis and many others like them, feed the fantasies of the super stud. Young men are hungry for sexual adventure, in whatever form it takes; they are up for it. The reason for all this rampant, unbridled confidence, is most of them they have not yet experienced **Failure with a capital F.** *So for this brief magnificent period in the new male lifecycle, the male hero's ego in all his glorious potential, still roams free.*

But in our new world of Post Patriarchy, an important change is happening around us. The message from all around is "be more tender ", "think more about others " "show us your softer feminine side." The new message to the young master of the universe, is to curb his excesses and over-the-top behaviour. Strong, arrogant and riotous is bad: tender, kind and controlled is good. The young twenty something male is bombarded by post patriarchal propaganda from magazines, newspapers, websites. In a popular English novel called "A Man and a Boy ", the twenty something male hero grows his emotional intelligence. Starting out as an ego centric glory seeker lacking in empathy for others, he develops sufficiently to take responsibility for the nurture and fathering of a young boy. The new message is **to be tender more than tough, giving more than selfish.**

The feminisation of the young master of the universe, is also happening through cultural concepts such as the metrosexual male. The metrosexual male is overtly encouraged to be concerned with his looks and appearance. He uses skin conditioners on his body and face, and a moisturiser. He has body treatments, massage and aromatherapy at his health club; in contrast to pounding the streets or pumping the weights in the gym. These are all self nurturing experiences previously only the domain of the female. He dresses and grooms himself to win female approval. The effect of all of this, is to soften his masculine hard edges, tuning him into the emerging experience of masculinity and a new balance.

In the movie Master and Commander, the ship's captain (played by Russell Crowe) is the old fashioned warrior. He is sailing off to find adventure, heroism and glory. He is also *connected in some way to his artistic feminine side and plays the violin. The human drama in the film, is in the relationship between the captain and his closest friend, the ship's doctor. Throughout the whole story, the doctor is anti war, an intellectual scientist, a healer, philosophically reflective and a deeply feeling man. He constantly challenges and taunts the captain about his leadership style. He confronts him to be more tender and human; to reach out and get emotionally involved and more attached to his surroundings and people and care for them. The captain repels his psychology, saying it has no place for a soldier of the sea. The film was a huge hit. The popularity of films and books, lies in their ability to both tell a story well and stimulate an important aspect of our psychology. This film explored dramatically, our current search for* **balance of the complex opposites of the young man of today**, *in this life stage. In a sense, the two characters of the film, are the twin aspects of the broader and emerging new masculinity, of post patriarchy. The story dramatises for young men, their new experience of masculinity and the new balance in their manhood they are now seeking to find.*

Commitment or Addiction to the Chase?

Gradually from his mid twenties onwards, a young man begins to face a profound emotional dilemma. I knew a young man in his late twenties, who was very successful. He had his own business, which he enjoyed operating and which gave him a very good living. Many of his achievement goals were already realised. He had enjoyed a lot of sexual freedom during his twenties. Now there was a more permanent relationship in his life with a young woman. He came to see me, because he was in a profound dilemma, about what was to be the next step in his life. He had become engaged to this woman. She was young, beautiful, loyal, kind, sexy and a close friend; but despite all of this he was not sure what to do. Part of him wanted to run away from a commitment, and stay successful, independent, emotionally and sexually free. He was stuck. Most of all he told me, he still enjoyed his sexual freedom. He enjoyed the thrill of the chase, going out and chasing women, whenever and wherever he liked. The sex gods were both very active and alive in him. The Love Prince enjoyed flirting, courting and charming women. His Rampant Sexgod, enjoyed seductive and freely promiscuous behaviour.

He had arrived at the moment in the new male life cycle when a young man is asked to begin **to properly grow his emotional intelligence.** *To do this he has to be prepared to trade off his sexual freedom, in order to learn about loving; kindness, attention giving, empathy, generosity, forgiveness. In patriarchy, this commitment stage that most men went through, was less difficult. Taking on the risk of commitment and marriage, a man knew that he was risking both entrapment* **and** *opportunity. Staying with one woman, meant connecting the sexgods with a single partner, and trying to stay loyal to her. However, if he chose the right woman, he could enjoy sexual pleasures regularly and be satisfied. At the same time, he had the* **opportunities**

The Lost Patriarch

to grow emotionally, as a partner, father and nurturer. So commitment and marriage, enabled the next step in the male life cycle to occur. To grow from selfish, sex seeking hero into a thoughtful, loyal, emotionally sensitive partner and father.

In the new male life cycle, this crucial transition of manhood is being delayed by a genuine crisis of commitment. Now the risks of commitment are much greater for a man. More and more men (1 in 5), stayed unmarried and living alone between the ages of 25-44. Here are two reasons for this behaviour.

1. *More marriages break up than ever before, so a young man looks around and sees that the whole thing is much more likely to end in failure and disaster. This scares more and more men away from commitment. They see emotional pain, conflict and financial distress all around them in the lives of their brothers, close male friends and male colleagues. They think: "no thanks, not for me; not yet "*

2. *Men remain more confused at this stage of their manhood than ever before. They still feel trapped in a continuing male identity crisis, of uncertainty. More of them can do their own homemaking, and so choose to live alone. However, this leaves them stuck in their own emotional universe, unable to take the next crucial step in their lifecycle.*

30's, Fatherhood and Families

These are complicated times to be a man: nobody really knows exactly what it means anymore. Each individual man's life is a current living experiment in the new mythology of manhood.

One thing is certain however: having made a commitment to a relationship of partnership, started a family and taken on fatherhood, a man now has to change more than ever. Men who still continue to put themselves and their own career before everything else, such as top sportsmen, lose out very heavily in the break-up stakes: 70% end up divorced! On a day to day, month by month basis, a man at this life stage now experiences a tense, ongoing, inner crisis of his masculinity and manhood. Is he a patriarch or a post patriarch? Is he primarily a provider or a nurturer? Is his heroism fulfilled enough by what he does and how he lives? How does the "psychological fit" of his relationship with his partner, make the search for answers to these questions, easier or more difficult?

The business of manmaking, does not suddenly stop with marriage or partnership. In many ways, it now accelerates it. In the new male lifecycle, the demands of fathering and becoming a homemaker as well as a provider, now challenge a man in his 30's more than ever before. Whilst still becoming fathers, less and less men actually get married in their thirties. More and more men, take on the responsibility outside of marriage. Over one third of children are now born to fathers who are not married.

This is a truly shocking change of familial behaviour; and the evidence is that it is increasing year on year. Where will it be by the year 2020? Or 2050? Or 2100? Let's look at the different types of fathers there now are in their thirties:

1. *Unmarried fathers, still living with their children and their children's mother.*
2. *Unmarried fathers who are separated from their former partner, but still fathering their children at weekends and contact days during the week.*
3. *Unmarried separated fathers, fathering their children on contact days, and living with another woman who has her own children from a relationship with another man.*
4. *Married fathers living with their children and wife.*
5. *Divorced fathers, still fathering their children at weekends and contact days during the week.*
6. *Divorced fathers, still fathering their children on contact days, living with another woman who has her own children from a relationship with another man.*

In the new male lifecycle, there are lots of contrasting family situations for being a father. I know men who have tried all six! Whatever the situation, the evidence is indisputable that men as fathers, are creating stronger and stronger bonds with their children inside and outside of partnership or marriage. Men who nurture in families, stay strongly committed to their children when the family breaks-up, and the circle of love reorganises.

Because of this new and growing male commitment to nurture and childcare, another fundamental change is occurring in the male lifecycle. It concerns what we have recently come to call our **work life balance.** In seminars with many men, working in very many different types of occupations, I have been told the same thing over and over again:

"I want to work less so I can have more time at home with my kids."

This is the primary emotional wish of the nurturing post patriarch. It symbolises the changing balance of manhood for men in their thirties, between provider and nurturer, hero and homemaker. It is at the very centre at the new psychological myth of manhood. To me it expresses the increasing desire of men to become heroes of the heart, as much as heroes of the workplace

At last, men can feel more comfortable about releasing what we call our feminine side. Not in some trivial, media created image of the New Man or the Metrosexual Male. But as actively loving fathers, elemental nurturers and homemakers, who relish and enjoy their daily intimate contact with their children. Men can find a new joyful and harmonious balance in their manhood, between their previously separated masculine and feminine psychology. This is the time for a man to make new deep inner connections. The old patriarchal male's nurturing feminine psychology, was locked away by his need to play the hero/provider role. Slowly, a way forward is emerging for men *in post patriarchy and it reveals exciting new opportunities for male liberation.*

Living in the 40's: Break-up, Burnout and Singledom

By the time a man reaches his forties, it is now normal for him to have experienced at least one divorce or family break-up with his live in partner. This is because it is no longer normal for a man and a woman to stay together for a life time. How many men and women do you know who got married in their twenties, and are still together in their forties? They are few and far between. The figures of break-up are disguised by the figures of divorce: 4in 10 marriages. To that, you have to add all the couples who never got married, but tried to live together and had children; and then separated. And then those that re-married with a further 5 out of 10 break-up ratio. So another event in the new male life cycle, is the profound shock and trauma of a couple and their family breaking-up. If you are a man in today's world, you have to learn to be up for it. Men will have to become better at forming support groups for each other, to help themselves through this now normal crisis in the male life cycle.

This is in addition to the now well studied phenomenon of Burnout. Burnout is the result of too much work, for too long, in a job or career of which you have had enough. You end up physically, emotionally and psychologically exhausted, cynical, depressed or angry. Burnout is more and more, becoming a feature of the new male life cycle. Companies, careers and professions, expect more and more of their male employees. They use up their human resources, with less and less regard for their long term wellbeing. At the same time as having to work harder and harder, men are also putting in more and more time in the home and at childcare. The result is that they burnout with increasing regularity. Policemen, teachers, doctors, nurses, company workers, the self employed; all have rapidly increasing levels of burnout that result in the early onset of mental and physical disease.

Along with the process of aging, comes the start of a decline in sexual energy and libido in the 40's. One of the great secrets of the new male life cycle still yet to be exposed, is the amount of sexual problems men now experience as they grow older. The most common is to do with their ability to get and keep a firm erection. When we are in our testosterone overloaded teens and early twenties, this is as easy as looking at a photo of a naked woman. Then we can masturbate two, three, four, five, times a day, enjoying a large and gloriously long erection. As men approach and enter their 40's, for many men a firm erection becomes much more difficult both to get and to sustain. One in four men admit to having difficulties like this, and the numbers are increasing and probably much higher. Changes in sexual energy and libido, are now an important part of the new male life cycle. Men need to start facing the truth of that. This is not an easy or straightforward thing to do for the sexual hero and horny god. It concerns a very *irrational area of our psychology, to do with male machismo and our primitive sexual manhood. We like to continue to believe that whatever difficulties may be going on "outside", we can still get a good hard on and "do the business " in bed. The truth is, when going through a divorce or break-up, or overloaded with pressure at work, or all of these things combined with the process of aging, our sexual manhood can become temporarily dysfunctional.*

The great cover up of male sexual dysfunction, is an attempt to try and hide men's sense of shame at the decline in their sexual manhood. The positive way through this 40's sexual problem if it happens, is twofold. Firstly, allow yourself to recognise and admit it. Then seek skilled help through sex therapy. Sexual counselling in combination with the new drugs available, will nearly always improve sexual energy and erection performance. Second, recognise that a man's declining sexual energy and libido, means a change in his sexual personality. This older sexual male, can actually **improve** *his sexual performance with a woman. Not being able to shoot off like a loose sexual cannon all the time, actually improves the satisfaction he is able to give a women, by becoming a more skilful, controlled and dedicated lover.*

For a man in his forties, getting to the new emotional and sexual territory of Midlife Singledom, is not an easy or straightforward journey. For a man, becoming single again after a lengthy period of life sharing, marriage and family life with a woman, is like suddenly finding yourself in a foreign country with no passport, unable to speak the local lingo and no map reading skills! Very quickly you have to work out where you are, what everyone else is doing, what language they speak, opportunities for enterprise and potential dangers to avoid.

Rule 1.
Learn to be comfortable with the emptiness and aloneness.

The first thing is learning to be alone. After years of partnership and intimacy, being accustomed to a constant female companion and the noisy comforting presence of children, you suddenly discover BEING ALONE. You sleep alone, get up alone, come home to an empty house, you cook and eat alone and you watch a movie on television; all alone. You now find yourself becoming overdosed, on the very thing you craved for most when married and with a the family as it was; more time by yourself. If you are not careful, you can find yourself drowning in a vast ocean of aloneness. At this point, a lot of men will rush out in anguish, searching to find an instant replacement for their lost family circle, ex-partner or wife. Afraid and freaked out by the emptiness in their new single life, they try to replace it immediately or too soon with another relationship. It is then that more life mistakes are made. This kind of emotional panic is so typical of male and patriarchal behaviour and has two motives: firstly to block out and deny the immense loss and pain, currently being experienced at relationship and family break-up: secondly to try and avoid the new reality of being alone,

The Lost Patriarch

and its potential for learning emotional independence as a man. Divorce and family break-up is a death; as a man you need to learn let yourself die in order to come alive again. The take another off the shelf attitude to new partners, wives, families and life, rarely works. The lessons have to be learned about love and loving, or the same male patterns will be taken to a new relationship. Each one of us men, has to face what we have been and what we can now become, in order to enjoy a better future life of our own making.

Now is the moment in your new single life, to face the fear and panic all men feel at this moment in their lives. It is the fear and panic that a man will feel, when confronted for the first time **with becoming fully responsible for himself in the world and on the planet**. *As a man, you will have relied very much on a woman up to this point in your life, to support and nurture you physically, emotionally, domestically and sexually. From that first desperate angry breath taken after the escape from the womb of your mother; to falling into the arms of your first love goddess; to creating a family with your partner or wife, you will have learned to enjoy the dependant comfort of HER nurture.* **Now it is time to grow up.** *At last, in your thirties, forties or fifties, you can embrace the opportunity of learning to become emotionally and domestically self sufficient.*

I am not saying, give up women or become sexually abstinent: (more on that later). What I am saying, is:

begin to wean yourself from the dependency on women that you have been conditioned into believing you must have,

from the moment you were born!

Rule 2.

Learn how to become a Domestic God

If you relied on your ex-female partner to do the washing, buy the groceries, clean the kitchen, replace the toilet paper, wash the loos, iron the laundry, vacuum the carpets, cook the meals, choose the colours for the curtains and bedding, wash the fridge, select the cleaning materials at the super market and defrost the freezer: now is your once in a lifetime opportunity, to become a Domestic God. Embrace it now and celebrate your manhood in a new way. You will grow and become more complete as a man and homemaker. The end of female domination of the domestic universe is at hand. If you were one of those few but increasing numbers of men, who slowly became a domestic god during the marriage/partnership, now you can learn to become an even better one. Most men are natural homemakers. Learn the many pleasures and deep sense of satisfaction that can be gained, from spending a weekend homemaking; shopping, cooking, cleaning, tidying, gardening, washing and tendering to your own home. This is more of the gloriously feminine pleasure of homemaking for men, that women have had to themselves for far too long.

Rule 3.
Discover True Sexual Liberation!

Learning to live alone in the new land of emptiness and aloneness is a very creative time. This is particularly so of a man and his sexuality. In marriage and long term partnerships, sex nearly always becomes involved in bargaining and trade offs between a couple. After the erotic excess of the early falling in love stage, a man will have to start bargaining with a woman. Most women, and research over the last two decades definitely confirms this, gradually lose interest in sex with their long term male partner. In the early falling in love stage, you were truly their prince and love god, with whom they were willing to dance sexually all day long. This brief being in love period, was only an evolutionary mechanism to pair you off and create a lasting bond for procreation. Slowly it dies away, leaving most men less and less sexually fulfilled with and by their partner. Women continue to masturbate and fantasise regularly about their sexual hero figures: film actors, footballers, pop singers, your friend from work whom they met at a party with you. But actual sex with you their partner, falls lower and lower on their day to day agenda. Unfortunately or fortunately depending on your view, it remains very high on the male agenda, throughout most of his life cycle; certainly up to and beyond this midlife point.

The newly divorced man in singledom, initially alone, has to rely primarily on masturbation to express and satisfy his ongoing sex drive. This is no bad thing, because when in a marriage or partnership, he masturbates often with a sense of disappointment or guilt. Disappointment that he is not making love to his wife or partner: guilt that he is doing it and thinking about another woman. Learning to masturbate as often as he wants, and thinking about whomever he chooses to think about, is an important stage in his new sexual liberation. Why? Sexual manhood begins in adolescence when we encounter our first true love goddess. She switches on the twin sex gods within us: the Rampant Inner Sex God and the Love Prince. But this first sexual liberation is an instinctive, hormone driven, psychologically unconscious process over which we have little or no control. We are spellbound and captured by her erotic power.

Now in our new older, wiser, post marital single state, we can begin to become more familiar with our twin sex gods and their highly contrasting power and energies. The fantasies we play out in our rituals of masturbation, can help us in this liberating process. Get to know the twin sex gods and the very different moods and energies they arouse in you. Learn to master them, rather than the other way round. When a man can begin to do this, he can have more understanding and choice about the kinds of women who turn him on sexually. Reflecting carefully on the kind of woman who he is now being attracted to, will continue this process of sexual self awareness and self knowledge.

Divorce is a death. This is very much the case with a man's sexuality. In a marriage or life partnership, a man learns to attach and channel his sex gods to one woman. Over the years of creating a common sexual language together, he and his partner create a sex life unique to them. When they separate, that sex life dies as well. This is terrifying to a man; or rather the twin sex gods within him. He may temporarily lose sexual confidence, doubt his sexual powers, and become uncertain of his sexual attractiveness to other women. He has to learn to begin again and re-attach his sex gods to another/other women. Initially, it is like going back to the early years of adolescence, when he was a sexual beginner. After the emotional disaster of marital break-up, most men seek out a **female sexual healer**. *This woman plays a very important role in both emotional and sexual healing. Many men seek out an older woman; she can combine soft healing sex, with the kindness and nurture his current vulnerable state of recovery requires. She is also sexually reassuring to his sexual prowess, enabling his sexual machismo to re-emerge. Her kind open heart and body, enable his sex gods to be reborn after the disaster of a lost love life.*

If a man follows these 3 rules, (for a minimum of two years after break-up), then he will have a good opportunity to gain genuine learning, and grow from the emotional disasters in which he has been previously involved. Divorce is death and a disaster when you are going through it. When you have negotiated its tortuous passages, it will provide deep emotional and sexual insights into who you are becoming. It is crucial that a man takes time to reflect with honesty and self awareness about what happened and why it happened. It will pave the way to a new self knowledge and independence, that can be truly liberating for his manhood.

Male Types: "IPOD MAN"

Ipod Man is a new breed of independent male, who is still learning the news lifestyles of post patriarchy. He works in the feminine arts as a film director. Having now reached his mid thirties, he remains unmarried, celebrating every moment of his sexual freedom with an innocent lust and love for life; and women. Ipod Man still hopes for the occasional presence of a paparazzi reporter, following him around sniffing into his very personal life. He imagines there might be a titillating news story for Film Quarterly, from his current girlfriend a young aspiring twenty two year old actress. She is hoping for a part in his next film project. Ipod Man's modest artistic eminence derives from when he wrote and directed, a moderately successful movie, when still in his early twenties. He has continued to turn out original, funny screenplays once a year ever since. This is despite a long sequence of rejections from producers and filmmaking companies, and their failure to back his original talents with hard cash. Even so, a fire of creativity and ambition still burns inside him and shows no signs of going out. As is often the case in the movie business, his career has been going steadily downhill, ever since his original early success.

For the last decade or so, Ipod Man has made his living filming adverts for the trendiest new Land Cruiser or making a pop video for the hippest on-the-way-up-band. This hip lifestyle has provided our hero's creative, financial and sexual desires with a good deal of satisfaction and fulfilment. Despite his long string of glamorous girlfriends, (an enviable dividend of his craft), stretching back a dozen years or more, he has somehow resisted the trap of emotional commitment. Fatherhood has still eluded him. Fiercely self reliant since he reached manhood, he has also been a success in enterprises outside the movie making business. His most recent enterprise, has been a company promoting psychedelic music festivals. These provide the otherwise well behaved youth of today, with a safe weekend environment to explore their transcendent inner space. They do this with the aid of hallucinogenic drugs, ritual dance and ear deafening pounding music. A Seeker himself, who toured India as a back packing nineteen year old, he was deeply affected by his spiritual journey through the planet's holiest land. A creative and spiritual life crisis looms over the midlife horizon for Ipod Man. He is reaching a stage in his life when he will need to make an inner and outer transformation: from a self seeking hero into a more compassionate student of wisdom and love.

CHAPTER 8:
A Future Vision of Post Patriarchy

Post Patriarchy and a New Mythology of Manhood

Birth is a bloody, painful, beautiful business. **Re**-*birth is also a highly disturbing and creative process. We men, are currently going thorough a* **profound rebirth of our manhood**. *The titanic waves of feminism and post feminism, have had profound psychological fallout across all spheres of life in our western culture. Fundamental change is now taking place in the male psychology of:*

Love Seeking, Sexuality, The Family, Work, Friendship,

The Search for Meaning and Happiness

The result is a deeply reflective challenge to the practice of all our past and current masculine roles, patterns and stereotypes of how to be and live as a man. There is no way back; and only an uncertain way forward for us men. To explore and learn to discover our changing experience of masculinity. Each one of us has to make our own individual journey, into the story of what now gives meaning and purpose to our manhood. Will our first masculine concern always about how to be a hero? That seems to have been our psycho-evolutionary heritage, encoded into our DNA. It spontaneously emerges in our boy play: adventure, conflict and dominance seeking. As we engage with post patriarchy, **our changing experience of manhood will also allow us to reach more and more into the creative and feminine inside us.** The result will be a new depth and breadth of purpose in the search for our emerging manhood. We are engaged in exploring and discovering a fundamentally new experience of manhood. Previously in patriarchy, living with the feminine, was almost completely the psychological territory of the female of our species. In allowing ourselves to reach into the sublimely feminine inside us, we men can begin to accept and flow with the gigantic processes of human and cultural change, in which we are caught up. These are disturbing but exciting times, when nothing less than the re-invention of the experience and meaning ourselves is our goal.

We men have evolved from hungry, scavenging cavemen, terrified by the huge and hairy monsters we learned to hunt and kill, with our shrewdness and animal cunning. This cunning has evolved into a scientific intelligence, now capable of harnessing the whole power of Nature, and exploring the infinite Cosmos. As we stand on the precipice of that great opportunity;

Who are we?
What do we believe in?
What are the beliefs and values that make us human?
What is the future essence of our manhood to be?

Let me begin this crucial debate by identifying some of the core concerns that lie before us. A concern for:

The Emotional Intelligence of Men
Fatherhood and the Nurturing Man
The Balance between Living and Working
Co-Operation between Men
Celebrating A New Global Connection
The Balance of our Psycho-Ecology:

The radical changes in the future of manhood, must now be envisioned and led by men for themselves. The 20th century was a century of **DE**-construction of our manhood. This coming 21st century, has to be one of **RE**-construction of it; by men for themselves. Women had to think and fight hard over the last one hundred years, to get themselves where they are, and want to be. We men now have our own opportunity to think through and feel for ourselves, what we want to change in our psychology. We must now start to take that opportunity with earnest.

For us men the search for transformation, has to start first at an **inner, personal, psychological** level. Only then, can it shift out into the external world of relationships, attachment, loving, family, work and achievement. To re-invent the psychological myth of manhood in our heads and hearts, we must begin by abandoning our stubborn attachments to traditional patriarchal values and ideas. These were the primal patriarchal qualities of what ' being a man ' used to be about.

> *selfish heroism*
> *relentless achievement seeking*
> *work and sport*
> *the selfish taking of love*
> *compulsive competition*
> *detachment from emotions*
> *the overwork ethic*
> *power seeking over women and each other*
> *sexual machismo and compulsive self gratification*
> *racial conflict and prejudice*

Those behaviours and patterns, belong to a psycho-mythology of manhood, that no longer fits with the fast emerging world of post patriarchy. All men between the age of 15-50, are now caught up in this intense transition of change.

This transition of change is re-inventing the very shape and purpose of our manhood.

A vast range of contrasting influences on the new mythology of manhood, are now effecting real transformation of what men believe their manhood is about. These new influences include:

Choice about the balance between working and living
Nurturing and bonding time with children
Searching for a co-equal partnership with women

*Becoming domestic gods and celebrating homemaking
Feeling and expressing positive emotions
Fathering sons into manhood and the New Masculinity
Celebrating both the imagination and intellect
Exploring the spiritual side of our psychology
Connecting at a planetary level with change*

These are some of the dynamic forces of change that are re shaping the identity of manhood, at a fundamental level. Many of us as individual men, experience this as confusing and overwhelming. It can bring increasing uncertainty and self doubt into our lives; about who we are, what our lives are for and how they should be lived.

This profound confusion about our changing and emerging manhood identity, can leave each one of us feeling unhappy and lost as individual men. It can seem like we are being asked to let go of the very things that **made us men**. These old fashioned beliefs, values, desires and life aims, shaped the identity of **patriarchal manhood.** They grounded us to our lives in a real and practical way. It is only over the last forty years that we have come to understand the male ego, and all its vulnerabilities, as fragile, shallow and something to be fundamentally re-shaped and reinvented by ourselves. This is because the softer more feminine part of our manhood, was suppressed and buried by the harder, tougher male roles we were expected to play in patriarchy.

In a peculiar way, we **men were as much imprisoned as empowered by patriarchy.** We were allocated the *macho roles to play: hero, warrior, provider, achiever, competitor, strong man/tough guy, the man who had to learn how to hide the soft feelings of his tender heart. We were as much repressed, as allowed to express the fullness of our masculinity. Once we begin to introduce and truly accept this softer aspect of our manhood, and let it come into our day to day practical lives as men,* (**in parallel to the traditional masculine,**) *things begin to take a more whole and satisfying shape. It is not an easy or quick journey to make. This is because what we are learning to discover is a new and fundamentally greater strength of manhood through a New Balance.*

The Fragile Tower of the male ego and what the old machismo was about, is being done away with and replaced. The old two dimensional tough guy, who beat up on others and the world in his search for success and glory, has been falling down in his millions with every kind of illness and disease it is possible to get. We are looking for ways to find a new strength, that will emerge as we learn how to hold together the opposites in our masculine and feminine nature.

<u>We men are forging a new alchemy of being that belongs to a future we are creating for ourselves.</u>

More and more men tell me details from their individual life stories, about their struggle to make the transition from patriarch to post patriarchal man. The most common theme in their stories, is their new and growing sense of freedom and liberation! I predict that men who make this transition of identity in their lives, will be happier, live longer, be more free from disease, enjoy healthier and stronger attachments with their children, and achieve greater wellbeing and work life balance in their lives. They will also be leaders of change in our post patriarchal culture, for other men to follow. We are living through only the first real generation of change in the core identity of manhood. This needs to become an ongoing transformation that is radical and fundamental in lifestyle changes. It will address core issues of male identity, purpose and compatibility, and will have to continue to evolve over another three to four generations at the very minimum.

The 20th century was the century of liberation for women. The 21st century will be the century of liberation for men.

A big part of a man's personality, resists change of this fundamental type. Our ancient, primal, heroic, masculine psychology is conservative. It wants to fight against the independence and recent and continuing empowerment of women. It wants to resist the softer feminine aspects intruding into male life. It wants to hold on to the patriarchal power it has had for hundreds of thousands of years. Power maintains certainty; change brings uncertainty and a profound sense of loss of control. The power seeking, conservative aspect of our masculinity experiences anxiety and anger, about the current radical changes confronting our manhood identity. This is the time when the softer, kinder, more generous and loving aspects of our manhood, must be given expression. We have to learn to overcome our fear about letting go; and allow ourselves to see what happens within ourselves.

How do men need to get more involved?

The vast transition of change in manhood identity, is happening all around us. It is happening so quickly that men often experience it as a cultural revolution beyond their control. If this is the case, there are still many ways in which men as individuals and in groups, can be more proactively involved as agents of the practical changes that need to come.

The following issues are in no order of priority, and represent some of the most important priorities for men to seek change.

1. The current structure of the working week for men, in most companies and organizations.
2. Equal rights for fathers, of paternity leave and pay, as currently provided for mothers.
3. Co-parenting contact and bonding patterns over the first crucial 36 months of the life of children.
4. The current structure of the working week

This "work, provide and achieve at all costs" psychology of manhood, ties men into their selfish heroic past. Men must recognise the fundamental re-organisation of structure of the working week, as the key to opening the radical door of change to their lives. Already some individual men see and understand this. Those who are self employed, *already enjoy an opportunity to begin this fundamental lifestyle change; a few are already making it happen for themselves. When businesses, employers and organisations, are prepared to assist in bringing about this fundamental lifestyle re-organisation, the changes that many men now say they want, will follow. These include:*

<u>Better work life balance:</u>
<u>Greater time to care for their children:</u>
<u>A co-equal partnership at home:</u>
<u>Equal bonding with their children:</u>
<u>Increased individual wellbeing</u>
<u>Sharing custody and care after divorce/ breakup</u>
<u>Escape from the Overwork ethic:</u>
<u>A new identity for manhood</u>

A small number of companies are now leading the way on this crucial issue of re-organising the work place, to enable a post patriarchal lifestyle to emerge. In these companies, employers expect their employees, (men and women), to work a maximum seven to eight hour day; then everyone goes home to their families. In addition, these and other companies, are highly flexible about men working at home whenever possible. A third initiative is, accepting whenever possible, part time male workers. This is the way forward, to achieve the fundamental lifestyle changes that more and more men want. Men need to protest actively to their employers and to the politicians, and support these few companies who already are showing the way forward for work and post patriarchal change.

2. The right for fathers, of an equal length of paternity leave and pay, as currently provided for mothers.

This issue is at the core of much of the psychological change, now going on for men. Research has shown for many years, how important the first thirty six months of a child's life are, to their psychological bonding with their parents and their ongoing child development. This research also argues that children cared for full time by their parent/s, develop faster than those minded by others. The principle of Nature appears to be, that babies and young children prefer their own parents to optimize their development. If optimal contact and care is good for children, it is good for fathers; and the father/child relationship. In order for fathers to be as available as mothers can be to their young baby and child, we need to find ways of giving men an equal period of paternity leave as mothers enjoy.

3. Co-parenting patterns over the first crucial 36 months of the life of children.

A radical re-structuring of a man's lifestyle and his work; and providing a father with equal paternity leave to a mother, will **equalize mothers and fathers in the bonding process**. *It will enable fathers to nurture and emotionally connect with their child, forming a bond of equal strength,* *security and intensity as that of mothers. This co-equal pattern of parenting, is particularly crucial over the first twelve months of a child's life. When mothers and fathers co-equally bond with their child, this bond continues to grow and develop over time with equal intensity. Fathers being much more at home in the first twelve months of their child's life, (for a significant period of up to six months,) gives the opportunity for what can be called* **the symmetrical family** *to emerge. In the symmetrical family there is a co-equal partnership between the couple, and a co-equal nurture and bonding process is ongoing with their child/children. The man and the woman, the mother and the father, increasingly interchange and share equally the roles of provider and nurturer. This is a fundamental lifestyle change for the patriarchal man and his emerging manhood. In patriarchy, the image is of the male provider leaving the house in the early hours of the morning, to earn the family bread. In post patriarchy: men take their children to school, then go to work for their children. They come home early from their work, and collect them from school to cook tea for them. They work flexible days and have a flexible working week, to enjoy maximum contact with their kids. When new babies are born, they also stay at home for months on end, on full time paternity leave. For some of their career, some men stay at home full time, all the time to be with their children if it is what the new co-equal couple decide together.*

The co-equal couple share a new work life balance. They balance the time they need to work and provide, with the time they need to nurture and care. Each of them makes important career and professional decisions, about what they want to do at work and what they want to do at home. **This is a post patriarchal vision of the future, of more balanced gender relationships within the family of the future.** *Men need to embrace this concept and psychological opportunity, and actively seek to bring it about. They can do this by influencing the organizations who currently shape the working lives of men.*

Men need to protest to their employers.

In the post patriarchy in which we now live, a huge transition of change is beginning in the nature of family attachment.

<u>Fathers who provide equal nurture and care to their children, quite naturally become co-equal attachment figures to them.</u>

Women insist more and more, quite rightly, that fathers take a more equal emotional and physical responsibility for their children. This liberates women to achieve and work at their own careers. More and more men are up to the new challenge of changing their priorities of manhood: becoming a nurturing father, balancing their own achievement seeking at work with being a nurturer and domestic god in the home. These fundamental changes in male behaviour and lifestyle, are emerging out of a new consciousness of manhood. They are resulting in a radically new psychology of family, formed around the co-equal couple and co-equal attachment between children and their two parents.

This is hugely positive and is a fundamental change in the way families are now forming. It also has enormous implications when families break up. It is no longer necessarily in the best emotional interests of children, who are co-equally bonded with each of their two parents, to live post separation, predominantly with their mother. **Their emotional loyalties will lie equally with each of their two parents.** *Fathers may have nurtured and fathered them, as much as mothers may have nurtured and mothered them. Why should the regularity and intensity of contact between child and father, suddenly and dramatically be interrupted? The consequences of suddenly making the nurturing father, an emotionally peripheral figure to whom a child is sent once or twice a week, can only have negative consequences for all concerned. Shock, anxiety, guilt, loss and anger, are the well researched "big five" impact responses of the divorced child. When mummies and daddies stop loving each other, the co-equally nurtured and bonded child, will respond best by being offered continuity of co-equal contact/nurture, between their two new homes. In this way the circle of love can be reorganized, with the minimum of psychological damage to all concerned.*

Stephen Duke

The Time of No Myth

Men have been living through the time of no myth. Everything is post: post feminist, post capitalist, post Christian, post patriarchy. Post, post, post. Now is the aftertime. Everything seems to have come and gone. We sit abandoned, on the vacant, barren secular plains of disbelief, longing, waiting, searching. For all of our previous time on the planet, we men have always lived under a great story; a sublime and sacred myth within which we have journeyed to and through our manhood. Every human culture has celebrated and lived within its own great story. A creation myth, a religion, call it what you want; each infused by its richly numinous, symbolic life of meaning. It provided everyone of us, with our sense of connection to each other, the planet and a profound sense of belonging. It united each of us with the universe, providing our sense of a deep cosmic connection; and through rituals celebrated with joy and ecstasy, a deep soulful experience of personal wholeness. Now that great story, and its rich symbolic culture has gone. It has been broken up by the relentless hammers of Reason and Logic. It is no longer out there for us to look at, to connect with, tune into and celebrate in our individual and collective experiences. We live and struggle in a confused world disconnected from our natural and spontaneous spirituality. An innate spirituality that has been part of our male psychology since the beginnings of human consciousness.

The Lost Patriarch

For us men, **Heroism comes easy: Loving is far more difficult.** *The journey through manhood, is the slow transformation from being selfish hero into a more compassionate being of love. This is a spiritual journey and has always been explored in sacred music, painting, poetry, stories, fairy tales, worship, prayer and myth. All these once vital, holy activities have become marginalized as entertainments. We go to the theatre or a movie as escapism, to temporarily distract ourselves from the empty meaninglessness of our lives. Now, all that we have to compensate for the loss of the cosmic connection is the urgency for more; the Overwork ethic, busy-ness, Television Soaps, Big Brother, Q magazine or shopping therapy. These things are material and psychologically shallow, not magical and mystical. Our immersion in them keeps us rooted and entangled in our senses, and our largely negative human masculine emotions: competition and insecurity rule, with anxiety, anger, self doubt and fear.*

But our masculine consciousness has far, far greater potential: to join with the numinous and the higher, spiritual transpersonal state of mind-being. Capitalism and the so called Enlightenment, Descartes' great error that we exist only to think, have all been murderous to the magical and the holy. They have split us off from our soul potential, perhaps forever. Here is a simple masculine prayer for healing:

> *I feel therefore I am*
> *I dream therefore I am,*

Stephen Duke

> *I imagine therefore I am*
> *I worship therefore I am*
> *I live in balance therefore I am*

The only possible way back to the magical sacred connection, is for each one of us to go it alone. To make our own individual journey, back into our Self. We have to explore and find our own inner maps of the New Balance.

THE NEW BALANCE

This means learning to take what we can find and make use of what we see around us, and bring it in to ourselves. All men are on a new journey; many of us self consciously seeking re-connection with the truly spiritual and deeply feminine. The future of manhood lies in discovering how to integrate a new balance of the heroic and the holy, the selfishly impassioned and the compassionate, the tender and tough, the material and the romantic. Striving for heroic achievement in the workplace, can be balanced with enjoying the nurturing delights of fatherhood and homemaker. We can still be creatures of Logic and Reason, whilst exploring and discovering the global imperatives of our time, ecology and the sacred connection. Patriarchy imprisoned us men as much as the women, upon whom it imposed our repressive controls.

Now is the coming time
of
New Awakenings
and
Male Liberation.

Men have their babies too!!

When my third child was conceived, I had what the Jungian psychologists call, "a big dream." I dreamed that I wrote and published a book, and that I composed and released my own CD. of music. Ever since then I have understood that we men are as fertile as any woman. The difference is that we men have our "babies" imaginatively at first, and then create them in the physical world around us. This male fertility has been responsible so far, for making most of what we have called human culture. Our programming by Nature to create, is just as strong as the female of the species. We men are naturally creative. Novels, paintings, buildings, gardens, cars, philosophies, political systems, theatres, bridges, symphonies, quantum mechanics, classic pop songs, religions, technologies. These are all products of the male mind, the male imagination and male fertility. The mind of the male of our species is infinitely fertile. Every man in his own way, is driven by this imaginative and psychological impulse to create.

To do that we need the space, that "cave", that every man needs somewhere in his life; his study, his studio, his garage, that special shed at the end of the garden. Every man needs that quiet, solitary space that belongs only to him. It is if you like, his womb, his fertile ground, where he can be at his most generative. Here he can sit and relax, and go outside what he experiences as space time, in the normal restricting sense. He can lose himself, and uncover himself. He can step outside that part of himself, which functions in the linear world of logic. He can allow himself to **play**. *In his special, solitary, play-space, he can continue to allow his childlike natural creativity to emerge. Doodling, with no serious intention, waiting for his mind to release in play, whatever he is able to make and bring alive. Inventors have their workshops full of developing innovations; painters their studios immersed in water colours; scientists their test* *tube laboratories; composers their recording studios and gardeners their landscapes and flower beds.*

The male psyche is infinitely creative.

What is each of us to do with this natural male creativity? How can we have our babies too? You have to go your own way, believing that you are pregnant with imagination, fertile with intellect and invention. Quite recently at other times in patriarchal history, a man's creativity was easily expressed within the culture in which he lived. Leanardo da Vinci was the last man in western culture, who comfortably allowed himself to explore all his natural creativity; artist, scientist, inventor, radical thinker. This is not so today. In our culture we are now channelled into one occupation. One professional training dominates our lifestyle. We are allowed to be a builder, a banker, a teacher, a doctor, to fix computers, or sell insurance. Think of mind in the round, seeking to become a complete circle as it creates, invents, and seeks to understand more and more things about itself and Life. There is a repressive and restrictive force working today on the male mind, seeking to make it impotent. To fragment, to limit, to split and so reduce this natural, rounded, potentially infinite creativity within each of us men. Resist it. Break through it. If your creativity is of the technical kind, when you are at a party, introduce yourself as someone who works in a bank, and is trying to invent a new form of microchip. If you are musically creative, sell insurance but express your creativity by writing symphonies at the weekend. If you are artistic, create with brushes when you are not having to earn a living or care for your children. Embrace your opposites, and so become rounded. Let your mind complete the circle it seeks to become.

Heroes of the Heart.

One of the most powerful images of manhood which survives on film from the 20th century, is of the great black American sprinter Jessie Owens. He is seen trotting around the running track with his hand raised in friendly triumph, at the 1936 Olympics of Berlin. Owens had just trounced all the opposition, including the vast array of blonde "Superman" athletes from the self appointed Masterace. He had won 3 gold medals in the sprint races. The '36 Olympics took place at the height of the collective male disturbance of Teutonic Fascism. Hitler and his group of murderous cronies, had planned the '36 Berlin Olympics to be a global demonstration that would show off to the world, the "glorious reality of the white blonde Superman." They had somehow convinced themselves, that the future of mankind was in their hands, and that this future was the future of their white blonde master race. The film of the Olympics, shows a brief image of Hitler standing with a look of astonishment and disgusted disbelief at Owens' triumph. He, the black American athlete, was clearly the supreme form of athletic manhood on display at those Olympics. How could this have happened? How could a black man, formerly a slave to the white man, and who's racial origins lay in the primeval continent of Africa, have trounced the future blonde Master race? The Fascists had no answer to *this question. So they ignored it. They moved on, trying to prove their point on a much grander scale. They had to be beaten in a disastrous world war, costing 60 million lives.*

The collective male psychopathology of Fascism, grew out of heroic shame and humiliation, the sense of male powerlessness and a deep emotional woundeness. The collective manhood psychology of Germany at the time, was in a disturbed and desperate state. Un-nurtured by their emotionally cold and remote Victorian fathers, regularly beaten and over disciplined as boys by them, they then died in their millions and suffered a disastrous defeated in the First World War. Their shattered manhood, sought emotional recovery and spiritual healing from somewhere. It took refuge in the fantastic heroic folk myths of their traditional culture. All patriarchal cultures have glorious hero tales, which celebrate the hero/warrior and his magnificent strength, bravery and power. Fatally for the fascists and for us, from those hero stories, they then created their own Superman Myth, and tried to impose it on others, in a modern age of science and scientific warfare. This resulted in the most shattering war of all times, and a merciless genocide of an innocent people.

It is crucial for us in our time now, to understand that this disaster grew out of an attempt to heal the psychopathology of **the wounded hero. If heroes become defeated and dejected, they fight back with violence.** *Post patriarchy is not the suppression or banishment of the heroic energy in men: men will always have to be heroes, or try to be.*

Stephen Duke

This great experiment of our time and post patriarchy, is in the evolution of male psychology. It is about balance and wholeness, integration and connection, inside, outside and in between. How can the heroic and the compassionate, the achievement seeking and the nurturing, work alongside each other in our daily life styles?

Is Soul More Possible in Post Patriarchy?

Many things have combined to kill off our conversations with the Soul. Logic and reason, science, technologies, disconnection with the earth, overwork and the compressing of time, too much material hero seeking. We have been living through a very Soul-Less time, and therefore it has been a very unbalancing time through which to live. Looking back, it is becoming easier to see that it was the last century of patriarchy, with all its unstable conflicts. **Patriarchy gradually killed off the feminine.** *Bit by bit the tender, humane, inspirational, creative, and the sacred, became more and more scorned and marginalized in our culture. Mostly by men! The masculine will always seek an artificial and unhealthy dominance over the feminine. And the feminine tunes us into the Soul-Full.*

What is emerging now is a new possibility of soulfulness from the New Balance. When the Masculine Force and the Feminine Force are held in true relationship, a sublime harmony naturally occurs. This is the simple essence of all ancient eastern philosophies and "ways of liberation". The New Balance emerges from the sublime harmony of the Feminine Force and the Masculine Force in integration and balanced relationship. From it, comes the possibility of great energy and great compassion, great understanding and great innovation. This is because the Masculine Force is made Soul-Full, by its harmony with the Feminine Force.

Post Patriarchy, makes this harmony more possible. It enables men to tune into their soul full feminine side more readily, and tune out of the dominant excesses of their masculine side. The New Balance is emerging, with the changing of men, and the new vision of what manhood can be in a post patriarchy. We may live in a culture of science and disbelief, but the urgent potential in men to connect with the sacred in them, pulses on. It means that we are still continuing to seek out in the New Age. We long for an experience of the mystical, the transpersonal or self transcendent dimensions of life. In a highly de-sacralised society like our own, the search for the sacred has never been greater! We search for it now in many ways: through participation in music, drug taking, falling in love, holy addictive sex, meditation, yoga, tai chi, complementary therapies and being in a sacred ecological harmony with Nature.

Changing Men, Changing Planet

If we men are changing, what are we changing into? Living in post patriarchy, we are changing and evolving into a new different male gender of our species. Each one of us men, is on our unique individual journey of self discovery. It is leading us on a new exploration of how to bring together within us, the great male and female energies inside ourselves. More than the provider/hero of patriarchy, we are also learning to feel comfortable with ourselves, by tuning into our creative nurturing feminine soul energies. The result is, men are finding their own "liberation."

There are enormous implications that flow from this; both for ourselves as individuals in our chosen lifestyle, **and for the world around us.** *There has to be a significant and powerful connection, between our emerging individual liberation as men, and a larger process of change and evolution for Man, the species on the planet.*

The transforming nature of individual manhood, and the evolution of our species, are both profoundly linked. A larger collective human process of change is at work. This collective process is concerned with nothing less than the future *identity and purpose* of our species.

There is some kind of planetary shift of consciousness occurring in our time. Each one of us men, is caught up in this collective shift of consciousness. This shift of consciousness occurring at a planetary level, involves the reorganisation of the balance of the Masculine and the Feminine Forces in our individual human psychology. Science and Spirituality, Reason and Compassion, Tribalism and Peace, Man and Woman, State Ideologies and the reinvention of new male Myth. These are the great human themes, with which we seek to find ourselves connected to and reconciled with

The Lost Patriarch

as individual men. We seek to develop and grow a deeper awareness and understanding of them.

As we find our own new balance of manhood, we can see a broader picture, and identify with more of the collective change occurring around us. Most importantly we can empower ourselves, to identity with new initiatives for change: within our families, at work with colleagues, in our communities, with other nations and peoples. As we change within, we seek more to change the world outside us. Patriarchy was a simple life script for the male. Whatever his class, colour or creed, he was a hero provider. He expected dominance more than equality, put competition before co-operation, self interest before compassion. He tuned into the harder masculine qualities of the male psyche. Post patriarchy makes the myth of manhood more complex to live, but with richer rewards. It makes it more ethical, more complete and more alive with the New Balance.

A New Work Life Balance

Men have a new issue to sort out, that is really a very old issue for us. We now call it Work Life Balance. Each one of us men, has to begin to find our own answer, to what is the right balance between Work and Life. We have to face one question head on; how much achievement is enough for me? Remember, as a man we are programmed by two powerful forces to want to achieve. Firstly we have our hero energy. This is our deep inner drive, inherited from our ancient psychological past. It drives us compellingly to want to make a difference, to seek out and take on a challenge. To overcome and defeat it. We all want to be a hero, or try to be. Secondly, even in our post patriarchal culture, we are still being strongly conditioned by social and psychological forces to be "a man", to achieve and provide. This means we continue to see each other too often as rivals, and a threat to each others manhood. These two scripts, one from Nature the other cultural, continue to combine together, so that we look upon one other as rivals to be defeated. Because of it, we are always trying to get ahead of one another. This rivalry before collaboration, difference before similarity, keeps us apart. It makes it far more difficult for us, to reach out to one another and share positive loving feelings to each other as men.

It is clear that in this country, we men suffer badly from the Overwork Ethic. We work longer hours then any other race in the whole of Europe. Research shows that on average we work an **extra day a week in unpaid overtime.** Other research shows the opposite trend. Some men are spending more time with their families and children, and are more and more involved in childcare. There are clearly opposing forces operating. Some men are spending more time at home and less at work, whilst others are working more and being at home less. So some of us are working more and more and others are working less and less. Those of us who are working less are exploring and discovering how to live the New Balance. We want to be more home centred, loving, creative and liberated from the overwork ethic.

The Lost Patriarch

The others are part of what I call the "fight back". This is a large group, probably still the majority of men, who are still trying to resist the unstoppable forces of feminism, the liberation of women, and the shift from patriarchy to post patriarchy. They are clinging on in true male fashion with determination, stubbornness and bravery to the old model of life. They are the patriarchs still hanging out for patriarchy. They are the men who get the diseases that go with overwork: burnout, heart disease and depression, that are still at epidemic proportions in our culture. They are the guys who say: "well, if we have to compete with each other, and now the women as well, I'll work twice as hard to stay ahead"!

Sometime ago, I worked as a consultant with a small group of senior policemen on this theme of work life balance. They had very different lifestyles. One was a crime warrior; if the heat was on he worked 90-95 hours a week to get the job done. He was happy to do this and was not prepared to discuss the immediate and long term consequences of doing this, for both his physical and psychological health. He also ignored the effect of it on his family and partner. Another was also very conscientious, and put the organisation first. He worked 55-60 hours a week. However he had become unhappy with this lifestyle and felt overloaded by it. He was experiencing physical and emotional symptoms of burnout. He also wanted to have more child contact and time for fathering. The third had sorted out a comfortable working lifestyle, and already achieved a work life balance.

He did his contracted hours and went home! He felt he paid sufficient respect and loyalty to the four dimensions of his life: his employers, his family, his friends and himself. He was pleased with his work life balance. Through dialogues with each other, change happened. The middle man started going home at the right time. He worked shorter days, and when he was called in for a job as an emergency, he took time off later that week. He explored a new balance between work and home. He began to eat a better diet, took up yoga and spent more time with both his family and his friends. His physical and psychological health improved within a very short time. He pronounced himself pleased with his new work life balance. In short, he became less overdriven by his hero warrior energy and more tuned into his desire for rest, relationship with others and a deeper connection with himself. He learned to combine the hero/warrior policeman with the nurturing feminine father and homemaker. He discovered something about the New Balance. Rather than making him less effective, it enhanced his potency for living and working, in all its aspects. The new balance he achieved, rather than diminishing his

Manhood in some way, had the opposite effect.

This is the prospect that awaits men in a post patriarchy, that liberates them from being over dedicated to their hero/warrior energy; not losing their potency and power to the unreal threat of the feminine, but reinventing themselves with a newly balanced masculinity. Over dedicated work warriors, sadly ignore the imperative of change and usually

The Lost Patriarch

burn out with depression, breakdown and disease. I was told the tragic story of an over dedicated executive in a large company. He worked for two years at a frenetic pace to land a new contract. As a reward he was told to take it easy for six months and move aside. Three weeks later he dropped dead with a fatal coronary when 33 years old!

These are the practical day to day themes of the new work life balance:

Spend less time at work
Become less driven by the work warrior energy
Tune more into the home
Develop your creative interests
Spend time by yourself
Respect the need for balance in health and wellbeing.

When we men learn to free ourselves from the overwork ethic, we escape from the conditioning influence of patriarchy. It damaged us by the way in which it imprinted its learning on men, imprisoning the male ego to thrust for the illusion of **over** *success.*

Exploring the fundamental issues of work life balance, draws men into the deeper aspects of the new manhood. Embracing a chosen work life balance which they freely elect for themselves, is a crucial aspect of how men are reinventing themselves. It is part if the new model for manhood we are experimenting with, and about which we are making exciting discoveries. It is part of the dynamic transition of change we are undergoing. It is future making.

Making Kinder Men

In the movie Apocalypse Now, a colonel-warrior-hero, (terrifyingly played by Marlon Brando), has gone missing, deep in the jungle bordering Cambodia. The Vietnam war is at its height. Rumours have got back to the US military establishment that he has "gone insane", and is carrying out acts of mass random slaughter. These murderous acts are not part of a controlled killing strategy, managed by military headquarters. They have decided that they are the impulsive exterminations of a psychotic. They take the decision they have to suppress him. A captain from special forces, is dispatched to track him down and : "terminate his command ".

As the film gradually unfolds, we watch the captain journey through the killing fields of a dark and savage war. Slowly, ever more eerily, he descends into the hell on earth, that can be made by human beings. Slaughtered children and their mothers, lie bleeding to death by the banks of the Mekong river, through which he cruises. The charred bodies of US soldiers hang from the trees, still burning after their helicopters have been shot down by "Charlie", the communist enemy. As the captain journeys further and further into this human horror, he slowly reads the diaries and letters of his elimination target, Colonel Kurtz. He tries to grasp the psychological process of degeneration, that has taken hold of the college educated, highly trained hero soldier Kurtz. How has he made the psychological journey from disciplined, decorated, warrior/leader, father and family man, to the psychotic slaughterer he has now become? The captain cannot make the dark leap of imagination, which the civilised mind must do, in order to get inside the mind of the mad Kurtz. Instead, he has to wait until he confronts him face to face, and then engages in a disturbing and tragic dialogue with him.

When he finally arrives at his destination, the captain (and us), enter a world of manifest horror. Painted primeval warriors stand hypnotised with curiosity, staring at the captain and his crew, who remind them of who they themselves once were. Severed heads lie scattered all around and strangulated bodies hang from the trees. Murder, torture, sadism, and indiscriminate cruelty, are the base instinctive patterns of this world that represents the dark heart of Man. It is a world of hallucinogenic nightmare, realised by drug taking psychopaths. For the captain and us, it is like looking far back in evolutionary time, and then being confronted face to face by the darkest shadow of the human psyche; the Killing God of Horror. Finally the captain enters the presence of Kurtz himself. Although he imprisons and tortures the captain, it is clear that the mad Kurtz is also seeking some form of dialogue and "therapy" from the captain. Kurtz is trying to reach out for some form of emotional, moral and spiritual redemption, before he dies. The civilised part of Kurtz's mind, recognises that he has been taken over (because of war), by the ancient, primal, *murderous shadow part of the male psyche. He shows us that human beings can worship any god, even the god of evil. He shows us that the god of evil, still battles for his place in the civilised minds of men and mankind. (It is after all, only 60 years, since 6 million children, women and men were slaughtered and gassed by one civilised tribe, in the name of a scientific progress described as racial hygiene.)*

The story of Apocalypse Now, is a parable of the psychological and spiritual progress made by men, and their humananising journey through space-time. From a monster of killing horror, who worships the gods of slaughter and murder; into something different and better. It stares unblinkingly into the primeval past and says: "this is where we have come from", and it asks: "where are we going to?" Without doubt, the story tells us that in contrast to our murderous past, our future lies with the psychological and spiritual Gods of Kindness, Love and Compassion. Behind the confusion and challenges now confronting the male gender in our time, there lies a great opportunity for further psycho-evolutionary awakening. Each man has to learn how to reach out and respond. The progress of each individual man, is linked inevitably to the progress of the whole of the species of Mankind.

Reluctantly Reinventing Manhood

Each person today, man or woman, is seeking to discover a new meaning and purpose to their gender identity. The roles they live and play in families, at work, in marriage, are no longer dictated by tradition. In patriarchy

The Lost Patriarch

this gender roleplay had become so well understood it was straightforward and uncomplicated. Men on the whole were thinking, action people, work heroes who provided for their families. Women in direct contrast, were child bearing nurturers who ran and protected the household. The simple division of roles between genders, worked well for hundreds of thousands of years. The liberation of women has tipped us all, into the transitional chaos of post patriarchy. Now women choose their emotional, domestic and sexual independence, achieve their elected work goals, and pursue their own intellectual knowledge and organisational power. In a post feminist world, they search for the new balance in women's psychology. They ask themselves: how much are we thinking, action achievers in the world and workplace? How much are we also child bearing nurturers who home make?

The same kind of fundamental questions concerning identity and lifestyle, now confront both men and women's psychology. Unlike the women, who actively explore their own agenda with excitement and enthusiasm, we men are approaching it with great reluctance and trepidation. We feel that something fundamental to our psychological wellbeing and survival, is being threatened or taken away from us. Why can we not learn to embrace the opportunity the empowerment of women affords us men? The truth is we have become imprisoned by the fundamental certainties of the patriarchal myth of manhood. The quantum shift in male psychology, demanded by female liberation and the new post patriarchy, tips us into a crisis of identity about what the manhood of the present and future can be. The hero, work warrior, provider, machismo driven male defends his manhood with an angry and terrified resistance. The two great psychological energies we describe as male and female, are currently at war inside the men of our species.

A NEW MYTHOLOGY FOR MANHOOD

Allow yourself to love yourself for your sensitivity and compassion, as much as your ability to compete and achieve

Celebrate games for what they are:
Playful, life affirming celebrations of male athleticism, not alternatives to tribalism and war

Become emotionally closer to other man

Rediscover a soul connection with the physical planet
Celebrate the music of many cultures

Suspend the overwork hero in yourself
Find a way to meditate and be still

Manhood and Wholeness

We men live so much of our life striving for the goals we have not yet achieved. To make things worse, so many of us also live in constant anticipation of the long term retirement, we either do not reach, or die soon after reaching! Meanwhile our true potential for living in the moment, continually passes us by. The full moment to moment joyous pleasure of being, which we can learn to

The Lost Patriarch

celebrate at anytime, eludes us. We exist in the future culture. It is time for a radical change of mindset. Somehow we have to make a leap: **away from the future and back into the present.**

This is essential before we can begin the search for a greater **wholeness of being,** *for which we all long and from which our current culture and lifestyle still so effectively blocks us. First, we have to work less. We live in the Overwork Culture. We men all struggle for much of the first part of our lives, to become heroes in the material world. This begins with our early hero play in boyhood and childhood, goes out onto the field of sport and in competitive games of all types, into the school classroom and within our male peer group. We take this on through our manhood into the organisation which employs us, or for the company we set up on our own. Our relentless aim is to search out the challenges, striving for ever greater achievements and recognition for those achievements. When we do not reach some, many or most of those plans and aims, we then judge ourselves harshly. Much of the time as heroes in the material world, we are also seeking control and power over others and for more material possessions. This material path, has become the normal and inevitable path for us to follow in the first part of our manhood.*

At some point in this hero seeking journey of the material world however, the hero inside us will be ambushed by an increasingly strong feeling or intuition. This feeling or intuition will slowly gather strength, as we progress in our *accomplishments in the material world. As the hero inside us establishes himself with some success, something beyond the physical material reality in which we live, will draw us towards it. This meta (beyond), the physical, will tune us into the much larger, universal energy of the vast Universe in which we and our planet travel. This is the way our manhood psychology is designed. However, in the time in which we have been living, particularly the last 100 years or so, it has become harder and harder to allow ourselves to respond, to this tuning out, tuning in process. A small part of our mind brain, the Logic System, has hijacked us, and insists that we stay focussed on only the physical world. It also insists to us that there **is** no other world, beyond the physical world which we see and smell and touch.*

If we learn to stop for a few minutes each day, something gradually happens to us. We begin to tune out and tune in. Or we go on holiday for a few days or weeks; or a few months on sabbatical, we then consciously work at switching off the Logic System. Then our experience of a reality beyond the physical world, can grow very quickly. By not doing, working, rushing, longing, striving, living for future goals, we can then learn to do simple things well. All of us long more for this opportunity of knowing greater peace and calm in our lives. The world and our lives as men, seem to have got away from us.

By sitting still, breathing slowly, listening to music, being close to Nature, concentrating on a calming image inside ourselves through meditation or tai chi or yoga, our mind and body change. They recover a balance and harmony. All of these kinds of calming, meditative activities, can allow our bodies and our mind brain to experience different waveforms and vibrations inside and around us. The physical-material hyper aroused cybertech world in which we rush around, keeps us constantly tuned into a particular level of mind brain energy and vibrations. We only need to find a simple method of keeping properly still to switch them off. Very soon we then experience ourselves tuning out of these vibrations, into different ones. Part of the huge imbalance in our culture, and therefore in each one of us, is the increasing reluctance and inability to do this.

The journey through manhood is the slow transformation from self seeking hero, into a more compassionate being of love.

This seems to be the natural order of human life, as a man. Born as we are to become selfish men, driven by our needy passions, to become work warriors, and search for our own form of heroism. We then seem equally shaped later in our lives, to grow on and become more balanced beings, capable of more compassion and love. As we gain some success and achievement, at what we each consider to be our goals in the earlier part of our lives, we then seem more capable of giving and receiving compassion in our hearts. A man has to do what a man has to do, before he can learn more effectively about love. It is a long and confusing journey. The changes from hero to a more compassionate being, are slow and difficult to make. Seeking out how to be a hero comes easy to us men: emotional learning is much more difficult.

We grow through the first part of our male life cycle under great pressures from outside and from within ourselves to "be a man." In patriarchy, our machismo, our self esteem, our very manhood were built around a very fragile psychological structure called "the male ego." It thrived on praise won from competition, winning at the expense of the defeat of others, self seeking achievement and overwork. In post patriarchy we are beginning to see a vision of a new mythology for manhood. The search for new meanings, and how to reinvent the male of the species, is only just beginning.

TEN EMOTIONAL COMMANDMENTS FOR MEN IN POST PATRIARCHY

1. LOVE YOUR FATHER AS MUCH AS YOUR MOTHER
2. ENJOY THE LOVE FROM MOTHER, WHICH IS EMOTIONALLY UNCONDITIONAL
3. UNDERSTAND THAT LOVE FROM OTHER WOMEN, IS EMOTIONALLY CONDITIONAL
5. LEARN TO CREATE AN EMOTIONAL CIRCLE CALLED FAMILY, WITH YOUR PARTNER
6. LEARN HOW TO CREATE YOUR OWN EMOTIONAL CIRCLE FOR YOUR CHILDREN, WHEN FAMILIES BREAK UP
7. LEARN TO FORGIVE YOURSELF AND OTHERS WHEN THE STORY OF LIFE GOES WRONG
8. UNDERSTAND THAT MEN WANT TO USE ANGER TO CONCEAL FEELINGS OF FEAR, SADNESS, LOSS AND FAILURE
9. ALLOW YOURSELF TO FEEL WHAT YOU FEEL, AND LEARN TO TALK TO OTHER MEN ABOUT IT
10. REMEMBER: FOR A MAN HEROISM COMES EASY: EMOTIONAL LEARNING COMES TOUGH

THE END

Printed in the United Kingdom by
Lightning Source UK Ltd., Milton Keynes
141283UK00001B/1/A